# *A Butler's Life*

## *Scenes From the Other Side of the Silver Salver*

by
Christopher Allen
and
Kimberly Burton Allen

Frederic C. Beil
Savannah
1997

First published in the United States by
Frederic C. Beil, Publisher, Inc.
609 Whitaker Street
Savannah, Georgia 31401
Web page: http://www.beil.com

First edition

PUBLISHER'S NOTE

This book is a memoir, and as it relates to the life of the author all the incidents herein are essentially factual. However, in order to maintain the privacy of the author's employers—past and present—names, dates, descriptions, and places have been altered.

LIBRARY OF CONGRESS CATALOGING-IN-PUBLICATION DATA
Allen, Christopher, 1957–
A butler's life:
scenes from the other side of the silver salver/
by Christopher Allen and Kimberly Burton Allen
p. cm.
Includes bibliographical references.
ISBN 0-913720-95-X
1. Allen, Christopher, 1957–
2. Butlers—Great Britain—Biography.
I. Allen, Kimberly Burton, 1961–
II. Title.
HD8039.D52G713 1995 94-24937
640'.46'092—dc20 CIP
[B]



This book was set in type by SkidType, Savannah, Georgia.

This book is printed on acid-free paper,
sewn in signatures.

Printed in the United States of America

# Contents

Preface vii
Acknowledgments ix
Introduction xi

1. Silver Service 1
2. Serving on Sea Legs 13
3. Moored in the Mediterranean 28
4. Private Service 39
5. Journeyman Butler 49
6. Lifestyles of the Rich and Not-So-Famous 67
7. Life "Below Stairs" 82
8. The Urban Cowboy 100
9. Coming to America 119
10. A Butler's-eye View of American Holidays 135
11. "Part of the Show" 148
12. Contract Butlering 167
13. The Long Road Home 185
14. Some Thoughts on Being a Butler 201

Bibliography 209

# Preface

The dimly lit pub was crowded and cheerful; sounds of the corporate class celebrating the end of the work week rose from the tiny tables all around us. Setting down my coffee, I stepped up to the dart board and took my turn: triple nineteen, eighteen, double eleven. The high score owed nothing to skill. In all cases I had been aiming for the bull's-eye.

"Keep your elbow steady; only your wrist and forearm should move," advised the little Englishman who was teaching me to play. I wasn't sure what I thought more charming—his London accent, or the fact that he was almost exactly the same size as I was.

My sister and I had come to this stylized Irish pub because it had a cozy, nonthreatening atmosphere—the primarily Yuppie regulars weren't inclined to hit on you—and the bartender made the best Irish coffee on this side of the Atlantic. We'd come relatively early when the place was pretty empty and, borrowing "house darts," had begun to play just for the hell of it.

Dart players are a polite crowd. As the bar filled up, the skilled players, their own darts in custom-made wooden cases, had challenged us to a game in order to tactfully rid the board of us dart peons. They had routed us in rather short order; and, thus chastened, we retreated to our table and our drinks. Still, in the course of the evening I found myself playing darts with one of the guys who had washed us out in the first place.

He was about as English as I could imagine—sort of a

cross between Dudley Moore and Davy Jones from the Monkees, complete with an honest-to-God soup-bowl haircut, cords, and clogs on his feet. I had no idea how old he might be, but he seemed so continental that I judged him (erroneously, as it turned out) to be much older than myself.

"So, what do you do?" I asked eventually, a typical Southern California opening gambit.

"I'm a butler," he said.

"A *butler*? A real English butler? Like Jeeves?" I was enchanted. "Who do you work for?" This was a nice area, but it certainly wasn't Beverly Hills. I was unaware of anyone who might be rich enough to afford a butler, of all things.

"I work for a divorced gentleman who owns a corporation," he offered—rather vaguely, I thought. I supposed in the butler trade, to name your employer was Not Done.

"What exactly does a butler do, in real life?" I asked him.

"In this case, I do everything a wife would do—except give him a kiss and a cuddle."

Christopher Allen and I have been married now for eight years, and I've since found his droll response to be a huge understatement. But I've also learned that it's a response born of lots and lots of practice, because "What does a real butler do?" is the most frequently asked of the many questions his occupation raises when people learn of it. And because they are legitimately fascinated—as I was—by his responses, I urged him to allow me to chronicle them by writing this book. Since the English inflection is so intrinsic to Chris's stories, I have taken the literary license of writing the story in first person so the reader can appreciate the "voice" of the real butler behind the image.

I should say, for the record, that I am not "in the trade" and never have been. But I have a high appreciation for top-notch service, even though Chris's unflagging execution of it sometimes awes me. I never cease to be amazed at what, to him, falls under the heading "all in a day's work." But although I rail against the long hours, I appreciate the fact that he does the ironing. And I now throw a mean game of darts.

# Acknowledgments

We owe a debt of gratitude to the following people, who have helped bring this book to fruition:

Sloan Harris, who took time out to advise me on publishing matters; Priscilla Dunhill, whose interest in the story kicked a long talked-about project into action; Pat Moran, for the photo session, especially on such short notice; and, most importantly, the "readers"—Jon Roberts, Pat Moran, Betsy Whitcombe Pedley, Eileen Obser, and Judith Callison —for their comments and suggestions.

Special thanks to Lyn and Bill Ross, who double-checked the accuracy of the British English and French terminology, and who kept us in line regarding French wines and locations; Alison Cornish, Chellie Roberts, and Marguerite Schondebare, the grammarians, for watching for details like voice agreement and parallel structure; my father, Jim Burton, for the precise, "anatomically-correct" line drawings, as only an engineer can do; and to our friends and family, for the support and encouragement throughout.

Cheers!

# Introduction

Perched on a stool in Mr. Carstairs' closet, I finished polishing the last of twelve sets of cowboy boots in preparation for his return from a two-month trip abroad. At my feet, fifty pairs of gleaming, newly polished, custom-made shoes stretched down the length of the eighteen-foot closet. Above me hung two levels of jackets and suits that I had already brushed down after unpacking them from dust-proof bags. On the opposite wall of the room-sized walk-in closet was a bank of shallow, cedar-lined drawers that held shirts, ties, and socks. The shirts, folded and stacked a few to a drawer as they are found in fine men's shops, had creases and would need to be ironed before they could be worn. But that was one of the many reasons Mr. Carstairs employed me.

My name is Christopher Allen and I am a butler by profession. Being a butler is something of a lost art, a fact I find rather curious. Consider this: People who lead the increasingly busy lives of the late twentieth century could use a "Jeeves" far more than when the trade was at its heyday in Victorian and Georgian times.

The title "butler" derives from the French *bouteillier,* or "bottler," to describe the chief responsibility in medieval British homes of supervising the wine cellar. As this was literally his job, the butler was not accorded the high position we associate with the title today. During the eighteenth century, as his responsibilities increased to include the silver, china, and glassware in addition to the cellar, the status of a butler rose. Still, he ranked below the land steward (manager of the estate), house steward (manager of all domestic affairs), clerk of the stables, clerk of the kitchen, chef, confectioner, baker, bailiff (who assisted the land steward), and valet (the employer's personal dresser and companion).

Over time many of these positions were consolidated. Combining the functions of valet and steward with his own food-and-drink expertise, the butler became chief of staff. He supervised the cook, housekeeper, under-butler(s), housemen, maids, and any other household staff. This was a delicate position, because the lady of the house was said to "run" the staff. A good butler, for decorum's sake, gave the impression of being an assistant manager, but in reality functioned as a manager, circumventing staff troubles whenever possible to save the lady of the house any concern.

Before World War II, there were more than thirty thousand butlers in Britain. However, whether or not they served in the war, many of the household staff were casualties of it, for afterward, to help rebuild war-torn Britain, huge inheritance taxes were levied upon the large estates one associates with "Brideshead Revisited" or "Remains of the Day." Employers could no longer afford to staff their large households, and so the sizable "servant class" languished.

Today there are only a couple of thousand butlers plying their trade throughout the world. Interestingly, although one tends to associate butlers with England, the United States and the Middle East employ more butlers than the UK by a large margin.

I've been a butler for over fifteen years now, which by my forbearers' standards is a relatively short while. In that time I've found that in spite of the decrease in what is considered "large" households, there are many venues in which a butler can be useful. In today's world a butler is more likely to do far more than polish the silver and open the door. My jobs and those of my contemporaries have included planning and managing large parties, booking travel arrangements, arranging for and overseeing home security, maintenance, and even extensive remodeling projects. Although some of us work for Buckingham Palace and other royal households, most work for corporate chiefs, foreign diplomats, entertainers, and others of wealth but no title. Some butlers even work for luxury hotels.

The job can be demanding, unpredictable, and subject to long hours. I enjoy every moment of it.

And just for the record: Jeeves, the archetypal "gentleman's gentleman" created by P. G. Wodehouse, was a valet, not a butler. And that is correctly pronounced VA-lett, not va-LAY.

# 1

# Silver Service

"Hello, Chris?"

The voice gave me a distant shock, though discipline assured I would betray no surprise; it was that of one of my former employers. I hadn't spoken to him in nearly three years.

"Hello, sir. I trust you're well?" We exchanged pleasantries for a few moments, then he came to the point of his call.

"I don't know if you remember, but my birthday is coming up in a couple of weeks. I'd like to have a dinner party, a formal one, and—well, you know Jorge works for me now."

I knew. I had encouraged the man, once an assistant barkeep at my favorite pub, to apply for a position at the gentleman's company.

"It's just that a formal dinner's a little out of Jorge's line."

Visions of the endless four- and six-course meals I had prepared several times a week for this man flashed through my mind. What on earth was he doing now?

"So I wondered if you would do a small dinner party for me, and teach Jorge how to use the *guéridon*?"

A *guéridon* is a portable cooktop designed for tableside cooking and serving. During my tenure I had overseen the remodeling of his kitchen and had built into his kitchen design a custom-made rolling *guéridon*, which looked like a cabinet. The *guéridon* was equipped with a single burner and compartments for several sauté pans, cooking and serving implements, oils, vinegars, liqueurs, and the like.

I willingly agreed to the request. We negotiated a price, which, interestingly, would equal for one day's work what he'd formerly paid me in a week.

On the day of the party Jorge and I discussed the party requirements and went over the menu I'd created, almost all of which we would do on the *guéridon*. After we went shopping, the lessons began.

Jorge was a willing student, but his lack of what I considered to be the basics of service training gave me a shock—he had never done tableside service. He didn't know how to lay a table. Unlike the cooking requirements I had operated under when in this gentleman's employ, Jorge didn't do main courses. He made soups and salads.

This was going to be more difficult than I'd thought.

After teaching Jorge the basics of *guéridon* cooking, we set the table for dinner. I took him through the fundamentals of setting a proper table, including placement of cutlery, glasses, and napkins. I set out the wines we'd use and explained how and when each would be poured.

When the guests arrived, I had Jorge greet them and offer drinks. I passed the hors d'oeuvres myself, so that I could anticipate when drink refills were needed and monitor to some extent the alcoholic and food intake. The party gave me the unreal feeling that time had stood still—I knew all the guests from previous experience. My former employer was in top form, which also gave me a sense of déjà vu.

After the requisite extended cocktail hour, we announced dinner. Meals prepared tableside are a production in themselves, and a *guéridon* chef, something of an entertainer. But Jorge's hands shook as he passed the plates, and he was not unobtrusive in removing used dinnerware and cutlery. He forgot to lock the wheels when he brought the *guéridon* in for the salad course. While everyone watched him prepare the hot dressing and toss it with the fresh spinach leaves, only spasmodic foot action kept the table from exiting the stage.

## GUÉRIDON DINNER FOR FOUR

Assorted Hors d'Oeuvres
Spinach Salad With Hot Bacon Dressing
*Steak Diane*
Braised Carrots in Honey
Sugar Snap Peas
Leeks
Boiled Baby New Potatoes in Parsley Butter
*Bananas Foster*

*Steak Diane*

- 4 fillet steaks, ¾" thick
- 1 large onion, chopped
- 1 lb. mushrooms, sliced
- ¼ cup butter
- 1 cup beef stock enriched with Worcestershire sauce, red wine, and one garlic clove, minced
- ¼ cup heavy cream or 3 tablespoons crème fraîche
- dash Worcestershire sauce
- cognac

In a large sauté pan, melt butter over medium-hot heat. Season the steaks with salt and pepper while butter melts, then sauté briskly on both sides. Steaks should be very rare inside. Remove from pan and keep hot on a covered plate. Sauté the onion in butter until it begins to take color. Add mushrooms and sauté until soft. Add a dash of Worcestershire and cognac, then ignite carefully. When flame dies, remove the mushrooms and onions to the covered plate. Make a demiglace by adding beef stock to pan drippings and cook until the liquid is reduced by about one-third. Add the cream and cook for one minute. Return the steaks, with onions and mushrooms, to the pan, turning them in the sauce, and cook to the required doneness. Adjust the seasoning and serve.

*(continued on next page)*

*(continued from previous page)*

***Bananas Foster***

4 slightly underripe medium-sized bananas, cut into ¼-inch rings
¼ cup unsweetened butter
¼ cup dark brown sugar, packed
1 tbsp. vanilla
3 tbsp. dark rum (optional)
French vanilla ice cream

Melt butter in skillet over very low heat; do not burn. Add brown sugar and stir until sauce begins to thicken. Add vanilla and banana, stirring to coat. Cook thirty seconds. Add rum and flambé. Divide between four dessert dishes and serve over ice cream.

Both my former employer and his guests thanked me profusely at the end of the evening, declaring the meal delicious and spectacular. But although the food had been a success, I felt the training had not. Jorge wasn't, and couldn't be, a butler. One of the things that distinguishes a first-class butler is his ability to wait at table. But more than that, a very real part of the profession is a butler's *presence.* Jorge did not have the presence to carry out the meal we'd just done, even had he had the necessary technical skills. For particularly here in the States, it wasn't just the meal one came to such houses for, it was having a butler—especially an English butler—serve it to you. I wonder if the *guéridon* has been used since.

People I've met throughout my career are generally fascinated by the idea of meeting an English butler "in person," and one of the most common questions I'm asked is, "How did you get into this trade?"

Many of the old style of servant class were born into it. Their parents worked in large households, and children were trained from an early age to succeed them. I had no such background. Indeed I'm not sure it still exists in England today. Although I never foresaw that I would ultimately make my living as a butler, most of my earlier jobs served as perfect training for it.

Home wasn't a particularly happy place when I was young. My older siblings had moved out; and after the sudden death of my mother, I was the only one left at home. My distraught father was unprepared to take an active role in parenting at this late stage. Shortly after the funeral, he came to my room and stood looking down where I lay grieving on my bed.

"Your mother's gone, and I don't know what to do with you," he said, gesturing awkwardly. "So as far as I'm concerned, you're a man. Do what you like, but I ask that you continue to do well in school, and not bring dishonor on our name." His pronouncement spurred me into action to get out and do for myself. So, in spite of the fact that I had just turned fourteen, I went to work.

My first jobs of any consequence were in the catering industry. I began my training in the restaurant of a large hotel, where staff were plentiful. In Europe, unlike America, working in a fine restaurant can be a noble career, an admirable and lucrative profession to which people aspire. Working one's way up in a fine restaurant can take years, as it means progressing through four to six different levels, all with French titles and special responsibilities. *Commis* were drilled in proper back-service. I learned how to fold napkins and set a proper table, but I couldn't bring a dish to the table until I was a *demi chef du rang.* Attaining the rank of *chef du rang,* I could prepare meals tableside on a *guéridon,* but I couldn't take a customer's food order until I was a *station de tête.*

Everything in a restaurant was done through observation. Nothing more than a series of glances from level to level would tell a *commis* that he should fetch a wine bucket that would be required by the *sommelier* (wine steward) on Table 24. I learned that "hands, feet, and eyes" make a good waiter —hands that were strong and adept and didn't drop plates, feet that were quick and able to withstand long hours

### Glossary of European Restaurant Personnel

| | |
|---|---|
| *Maître d'hôtel* | Manager of the restaurant; responsible for staffing and scheduling. Interfaces with the head chef in the kitchen to determine menus |
| *Assistant manager (2–3)** | Makes reservations, greets customers at door, prepares bills |
| *Sommelier* | Recommends, opens, and serves all wines, aperitifs, and digestifs |
| *Station de tête (2–3)* | With assistant manager, seats parties, explains the menu, and takes food order |
| *Chef du rang (2 per station de tête)* | Tableside food preparation on a *guéridon*; does most of the serving |
| *Demi chef du rang (1 per chef du rang)* | Backs up *chef du rang* in table service; responsible for perfectly set tables and stocking of the *guéridon* |
| *Commis (1 per station)* | Busboy/go-for; makes sure tables are set up and cleared and waiter stations are stocked, cutlery is polished, and napkins are folded; can remove plates from table, but not serve anything |

*Number of employees per shift for seating of 150

of standing, and eyes that were observant and able to anticipate the requests of a customer.

"Still too shaky. Try again," coached the *chef du rang* as I, a mere *commis*, attempted to present him with a serving of matchboxes during a break.

I was practicing silver service, the ability to deftly serve with one hand by using a large spoon and fork rather like chopsticks, while holding a platter in the other. Silver service differed from plate service, where a meal is presented on a plate prepared in the kitchen, and was used a great deal in the finer European restaurants. As the ability to perform silver service was critical to our getting ahead, we *commis* would practice picking up coins, matchboxes, salt cellars, or a customer's leftovers—whatever we could lay hands (or cutlery) to.

Regardless of one's position in the restaurant hierarchy, because all tips were pooled (called the *tronc* system) it was in everyone's interest to provide superior service. At the end of the week, the largesse was counted and each level was allocated an agreed-upon percentage. For example, the six *chef du rangs* at one restaurant I worked for took thirty percent of the *tronc*, divided between them; the *commis*, five percent; the *maître d'*, twenty percent; and so on. In addition, the *maître d'* watched the stations, and if a particular station had been really superior, those working it would receive a bonus. This created teamwork and motivation, showing me another dimension to the job.

In addition to the waiting skills, which have proved to be invaluable in my career, I found working in restaurants could be quite a cultural learning experience. I was working as a *station de tête* in the Heathrow Hotel when I got my first taste of the culinary communication gap.

An Arab prince was a guest of the hotel for five days. At the height of the oil crisis in the 1970's, the wealthy Arab oil barons traveled extensively throughout Europe and were known to tip lavishly. Consequently all the head waiters begged the *maître d'* to seat the prince at their station and, to my joy, one night I was given his table.

The prince was a big, florid man in flowing textured robes. The tip of his long nose was nearly buried in a thick charcoal-colored moustache. His hands, weighted down with elaborate gold rings, moved continually, as though he was fanning away unseen insects. Waving away the menu without looking at it, he ordered a steak, well done.

Because I wanted everything to be just perfect for this member of visiting royalty, I took the order to the kitchen myself and told them for whom they were preparing it. The chef gave the order to the grill cook, and when I brought the steak out, it was a masterpiece—a twelve-ounce fillet, well seared on the outside, firm to the touch, a perfect "well done."

The prince's heavy black moustache began to twitch as I set the plate before him. "No, no, no, no, you don't understand," he said. "I want steak well done. Well done."

My face red, I took the steak back to the kitchen and communicated the request. Ten minutes later I was back, with a much smaller, darker piece of meat.

"No, no, no, no. Well done. More well done."

The chef looked at me in disbelief when I reappeared. Taking the steak, he literally threw it at the grill chef. "Cremate it!" he snapped.

Twenty minutes later I brought forth a small blackened object about the size of a bar of soap. The once-lovely piece of meat had been reduced to a four-and-a-half ounce disk of charcoal.

The prince beamed as I set it down before him. "Ah! This looks wonderful, wonderful," he said, clapping his hands.

In a somewhat strangled voice, I asked him if I could bring him anything else.

"Yes, yes. Some Worcestershire. And Tabasco, if you please."

To my horror, upon receipt of the condiments, he emptied a quarter of the bottle of Tabasco sauce over his plate. His small black steak swam in it.

I couldn't watch him eat it. I slunk away, certain that his visit had been upset by my ignorance. It was all I could do to return to his table to offer coffee and sweets.

"That was a most wonderful steak," he said to me with a broad, toothy smile. "Please give the chef my compliments."

His bill, including his wine and the tax, came to £85. On top of it, he tipped us £100.

I had the opportunity to perfect my silver service at the Cock Pit, a five-star restaurant in Eton. On the Thames facing Windsor Castle, Eton is the site of the famous Eton College, which is not a college in the American sense of the word but actually a very exclusive boys' prep school for well-to-do and titled sons of the aristocracy.

Built in the 1420's, the Cock Pit had originally featured a cock-fighting arena as a source of entertainment. It still remained in an adjacent building, a circular recessed arena some twelve feet in diameter surrounded by scarred oak planking. Because the cocks had worn metal scimitar-like attachments on their spurs, the floor of the fighting arena was comprised of lamb's knuckle-bones in order to give the birds better purchase when jumping. It was rumored that there was a tunnel, now bricked up, which ran from the arena under the Thames to Windsor Castle, in order to allow gambling-minded royalty to sneak over.

In the five hundred and fifty years since the Cock Pit's construction, the streets of old Eton had gradually been raised, with the result that now, in order to enter the restaurant, one descended four steps and ducked under a lintel made of heavy oak, much darkened and worn with age. Inside, reflecting the fact that our ancestors were shorter than men today, the ceiling height was a mere seven feet, with fifteen-inch cross-beams that read "Duck, or Grouse!" reducing the head height even further. Because of this, my five-foot-two height was actually an advantage, but it became automatic to caution, "Mind your head, sir," every ten or twelve steps.

In spite of its notorious beginnings, the ambience of the Cock Pit was very elegant. Heavy oak tables were draped with thick white damask linen from which the polished old silverware gleamed by the light of the candles, and pre-dinner cocktails were served in large silver chalices in private rooms upstairs. Whatever could be made tableside was.

At the time, I had progressed as far as *station de tête*, but because of the Cock Pit's more stringent standards, I began there as a *chef du rang*, working under a *station de tête* by the name of Henri.

"Christophe, the gentleman at Table 16 would like zabaglione," Henri directed. "A good opportunity for you to practice."

I groaned inwardly. Zabaglione is an egg yolk-based cream made with sugar and Marsala wine, served in a stemmed glass with a biscotti wafer. Making it on a *guéridon* required whisking the mixture by hand over a double boiler until it formed stiff peaks, a process that took nearly five minutes. By the time proper consistency had been reached, one's arm felt ready to fall off. In the six weeks I had been at the Cock Pit, every order of zabaglione had been deflected to me so that I could "practice."

"But I know how to make zabaglione," I said.

"One can never have enough practice," Henri smiled.

Henri was in his mid-fifties, quite bald, and inclined to sweat under pressure. And because service at the Cock Pit was regarded as top of the line, Henri considered it imperative that we do anything possible to make the customer's visit an exceptional one. Sometimes that "anything" was put to the test.

One January afternoon we had a reservation for an middle-aged gentleman named Mr. Baddington, who was taking his secretary, Miss Fey, to lunch on her birthday. Miss Fey was in her twenties, with long legs, a short skirt, and a blouse that showed off her not insubstantial bustline. When she placed her handbag beneath her chair, Mr. Baddington, Henri, the *maître d'*, and several businessmen in the vicinity were able to appreciate Miss Fey's ample charms.

At Mr. Baddington's request, we had arranged for a large wrapped box of chocolates at her place, and we had ready for presentation a spectacular bouquet of flowers. The bouquet, which stood nearly three and a half feet high and over two feet wide, was made up of the most exquisite hothouse flowers that could be had. But when Henri presented them to her, she pouted.

"Oh blimey, I haven't got a vase or anything. Wot am I gonna put 'em in?"

Mr. Baddington motioned me over.

"Isn't there a shop down the way, or something?" he asked. Without taking his eyes off of his companion, he handed me two twenty pound notes. "Please go and buy the lady a vase for her flowers."

I had no idea what sort of a vase he had in mind, nor what he wished to spend on it. The shop in question dealt in fine china, much of it antique. I ran there and explained my quest to the shop owner.

"There isn't anything in this shop for less than eighty pounds," she said with a sniff.

Outside, I looked frantically up and down the street. There were tea shops and pubs and small hotels, but nowhere that might sell a large vase. I was rehearsing how I'd explain my failure to Mr. Baddington when I spied the perfect solution in the corner of the tea shop next door. It was tall and fairly narrow, had a painted Chinese-style design—and was loaded with umbrellas. I ran back to the Cock Pit, washed and dried my purchase in the kitchen, and hoped neither Mr. Baddington nor Miss Fey would recognize its former function.

When I returned, he was toasting Miss Fey with champagne as she twittered over her oysters. She exclaimed over the vase, pronouncing it satisfactory: "It'll just match my settee." Then she asked for a prawn cocktail, being "ever so fond of prawns."

The meal continued with Beef Wellington *à deux,* served with truffles, imported asparagus, and baby new potatoes, complimented by a very expensive French claret. With each new glass, Mr. Baddington toasted his flushed and increasingly giggly dining companion.

Under normal circumstances, Henri, as *station de tête,* would have sat the couple, explained the menu, and taken their order, then spent the remainder of their visit unobtrusively watching their table to make sure everything was at hand. But during Mr. Baddington's meal, the restaurant caste system was thrown completely out of whack. The entire station was kept running. He wanted a Côtes du Rhône so Miss Fey could sample the difference. Then he wanted an order of escargot so that she could try that. Every hour he would toss me his keys so that I could move his Rolls Royce, as parking in Eton was metered and he didn't want a ticket.

At one point I passed Henri in the corridor, bringing Mr. Baddington a *digestif.* His forehead, creased with worry, shone as though it had been waxed.

"I don't know what I'm going to do if this fellow doesn't go soon," he muttered. "I'm just about all in."

Some three hours later they finished with *profiterôles* and espresso, by which time Mr. Baddington and Miss Fey were the only patrons left in the restaurant. I was coming back to the table with another espresso as Henri leaned over to refresh Mr. Baddington's Amaretto. The latter had apparently noticed Henri's propensity for perspiration.

"You're a sweaty fellow. Here," he grinned, slapping a fifty pound note on Henri's forehead. "Keep that on your head for five minutes, and it's yours."

Henri started to protest, but then straightened slowly and backed carefully away from the table. The *demi chef du rang*, myself, and the two *commis* all held our breath as we moved carefully by him, clearing away.

"Done!" Mr. Baddington exclaimed. Henri peeled the bill from his forehead with clammy hands and, regaining his composure, tucked the bill into his jacket with a bow. "Thank you, sir."

Because Mr. Baddington's bill was well over four hundred pounds and he tipped handsomely, we didn't even insist that Henri add his bonus to the *tronc*.

In fact, when we got off duty, we toasted Miss Fey too!

# 2

# Serving on Sea Legs

*Everybody has a hungry heart,* sang Bruce Springsteen over London's Capitol Radio. Humming, I reconciled the purchase orders on the adding machine, tapping in the sums in time with Springsteen's rolling piano.

It was the manager's day off, and I was in the office of the Co-Op supermarket going over the accounts. I had to admit, things were going well in my new job. Certainly the hours were more regular, which was why I'd made the switch from restaurant work. And although I'd been employed only a few months with the Co-Op, the manager was training me to take over his position when he retired next year. To that end I was happily learning the considerations of butchery, purchasing, stock control, and wastage, in addition to the management essentials of organization, scheduling, and bookkeeping. My prospects were good and I thought I had my future all taped out. The benefits of being a manager would be great. I would qualify for a company car and, even better, a two-bedroom company-owned house at a rate of £8 per week. This was astonishing, as the going rate for a two bedroom flat at that time was £60 per week.

Even so, I couldn't shake the feeling that something was missing.

The disk jockey interrupted my thoughts. "Here's a job opportunity you don't see very often, lads," he said. "'Looking for able-bodied young man, aged sixteen to eighteen, to work as a steward/deckhand on a privately owned, Mediterranean-bound ocean-cruising luxury yacht. Presently moored in London. Call this number for particulars."

I had the number dialed before the advert was even off the air. Unfortunately, the voice at the other end told me to mail my *curriculum vitae*—what Americans call a résumé—and gave me a berth number on Lambeth Pier as an address.

There would be lots of applicants for such an exciting job. Why be just a name? True, they wanted someone eighteen years old, while I was twenty-one, but I looked young. So for the first and only time in my working life, I feigned illness and left work early.

Lambeth Pier juts into the east side of the Thames, opposite the Houses of Parliament. Once there, I needed no directions as to the yacht in question. Moored proudly at the pier in front of Lambeth Palace bobbed a sleek, gleaming white, eighty-five-foot motor yacht. On the deep-ocean blue funnel, a lavish gold insignia reflected the morning sunlight. As I stood on the Embankment and stared at it, I thought it the most beautiful thing I'd ever seen.

The entrance to the docks was guarded by a big iron-barred gate with sharp spikes and a sign that warned NO ENTRY, rendered somewhat ineffective by being wide open. Taking a deep breath, I walked down the fall of the pier, unsure of just how to make myself known to the boat's occupants.

A heavy Midlands accent hailed me, sparing me the dilemma. "Kin 'elp ya?"

Looking up, I saw a wiry, dark-haired man in need of a shave. "Have you filled the position for a steward?" I asked.

"No, still taking applications."

"Well, I—er, just happened to be passing, and I wondered . . . "

"Oh. Well, git on up, lod. That'll be the captain ye're wanting. Coom aboard." With that, he gestured to the stairs, which I mounted hastily, before he could think the better of it.

"Rob Gilmartin," he said, wiping his hand on his sweat-stained T-shirt before offering it to me. "Chef."

I blinked. With his shaggy hair and jeans, he didn't much look like the chefs I'd worked with previously. "Christopher Allen," I told him. "Prospective steward."

I followed him down a spotless teak deck bordered by teak handrails that shimmered under many coats of varnish, through the wheelhouse and past a pristine galley that bore no resemblance to its occupant. As we stepped down into the lounge—or saloon, in boat parlance—I couldn't help but stare.

The room bore more of a resemblance to a five-star hotel than a boat. The walls were paneled in exquisite African zebra wood, and the powder blue wall-to-wall carpet under my feet was easily two inches thick. In front of me a round glass-topped table would seat six people. To the right, banquette seating with storage under the seats lined two adjacent sides of the room, fronted by a highly polished teak coffee table with inlaid brass edging. On one wall a built-in marble-topped sideboard and glass cupboard spotlighted Waterford crystal, each glass in its own custom-cut hole, and luminous pearl-white china monogrammed in gold with the same insignia I had noticed on the funnel. Gold-plated rods went through the handles of the drawers so they wouldn't move when the ship was at sea. The drawers, I later learned, contained gold-plated silver cutlery.

"Siddown, I'll be back in a minute," my guide said, heading for a stairway that apparently led to the crew's quarters in the forward end. Ignoring the five steep steps, he took hold of the handrails and swung himself down, calling "Skipper, this boy's coom about the job."

Captain John Anderson's well-trimmed moustache was stained yellow in the center with nicotine and, although thick and blonde on the sides, few wisps of hair remained on the top of his head. In contrast to the chef, he was clad in full dress uniform and he looked like a pilot. His black blazer was adorned with gold buttons and stripes above the cuffs, gold-braided epaulets enhanced the shoulders, and the emblem on the breast pocket read RYCC, for Rainbow Yacht Charter Company. But years of experience in restaurants and pubs had taught me how to spot an alcoholic, and the man who took my outstretched hand bore all of the signs. His bright red nose was road-mapped with a myriad of blue veins; even indoors, he wore thick, smoked glasses that hid his eyes. I put him at between fifty-five and sixty years old; I later learned he was thirty-seven.

I introduced myself and explained my presence, and we sat down. After a few stilted questions, he stood up and headed for the bar cupboard, in spite of the fact that it had just gone eleven o'clock in the morning.

"Drink?"

"Oh, no sir. I make it a point never to drink at interviews," I said. Seeing his face sag, I added quickly, "although I know a great little pub just round the corner, if you'll permit me to buy you a morning beverage, as a 'thank-you' for seeing me."

Behind the glasses the bleary eyes lit up, and off we went. I bought him three double Bacardi and cokes in the space of half an hour, and the job was mine.

I joined the crew of the *Rainbow* in time to prepare for cruising season, which ran from April through late September. In addition to myself, the chef, and the captain, there was another steward named Gary aboard.

Owned by a gentleman called Mr. Griffith, who was in the paper decorations and novelties business, the *Rainbow* could sleep eight people; ideally, two couples plus the crew. In the aft quarters, there was a master stateroom with a queen-sized bed, and another guest stateroom containing two single beds. Both staterooms featured bathrooms with cast-iron tubs and gold-plated fixtures. The boat was often used for corporate entertaining, with the first parties of the season beginning in France. Shortly after I hired on, we crossed the English Channel and sailed to Le Havre at the mouth of the river Seine, on which we would continue up to Paris.

In the absence of guests, the majority of my responsibilities on board the boat would be housekeeping and seaman's duties. We cleaned and polished incessantly, adding coat after coat of varnish on the handrails, oiling and buffing out the paneling in the saloon, keeping the teak decks immaculate. The tables, particularly those in the saloon, were polished every day, and the powder blue carpet was raked four times a day when guests were expected, once a day if not. Additionally I learned seamanship—how to tie the knots required to get us through the six locks between Le Havre and Paris, what the call signals meant, how to navigate, how to take a watch, and how to read a radar screen.

From Le Havre it took us six days to meander up the river to Paris, where we were duly assigned our berth at the Touring Club of France, a mooring for private yachts and barges below the bridge of Alexandre Trois. Each year the *Rainbow* had the same berth, located about two hundred feet away from the bridge, where it faced the western side of Paris and overlooked the Place de la Concorde. Our locale couldn't have been more favorable in my eyes; my first time in Paris, and here we were, right in the heart of it. When night fell the City of Lights came alive and the city shimmered under thousands of stars. It was like a dream. But when I said as much to Rob, he snorted.

"Dream? That's just what it isn't. Just wait till you try to get some kip, mate. That's the Champs Élysées over there, and the French drive on their horns going round it, no matter what time it bloody well is. Then there's the *bateau mouches*. They're those 130-foot converted barges over there, and they give visitors a dinner cruise of Paris." I learned later how that affected us. In order to light up the various attractions along the Seine, the *bateau mouches* were armed with powerful spotlights that frequently illuminated our windows, piercing the darkness with the intensity of a police raid.

In Paris the *Rainbow's* primary purpose was to provide a location for the company's French sales personnel to hold receptions for their potential buyers. The parties were organized by the very capable Marie-Louise, secretary to the president of the French arm of the decorations company. The sales people wanted these clients to order large quantities of Christmas decorations, and our job was to facilitate their efforts by giving the clients anything they wanted. To that end Marie-Louise would arrange for the purchase of the food and booze and, while the former would be delivered, the skipper would pick up the wine and champagne directly from the vineyard. The alcohol stores for the entertainment season included a twenty-five liter barrel each of red and white wine, twenty cases of champagne, a case each of scotch, gin, and vodka, a half case of rum, and all the appropriate mixers.

Each party began at sunset. Dressed in my black *Rainbow*-crested jacket, white trousers, and deck shoes, I would serve drinks to eighty-five or so guests while we cruised up the Seine around the Île de la Cité. Then, moored again at the Touring Club, we would break out the hors d'oeuvres and continue to keep the drinks flowing until late in the evening.

The more parties we did, the more I came to appreciate one salient point—the French drank wine only when they were paying for it. When the booze was free, the men drank scotch, and the women, champagne. After two of these parties, I had blisters on my hands from the number of bottles of champagne I was opening each night. After three parties, we ran out of both.

"I can't possibly get someone out there today to pick up more champagne," Marie-Louise told us when informed of our plight. "I'll phone in the order, and you'll have to go."

This was an unexpected treat. Rob, the skipper, and I took a two-liter Renault and drove two hours to the vineyard in Rheims to replace our stock of champagne.

The small vineyard was tucked into rolling hills of lush green grapevines, and as we pulled into the yard, one of the owners bustled out to greet us. She was a plump, smiling woman of indeterminate years, and she introduced herself as Madame Bonheur. Her hands, as she grasped ours, were rough and strong, and her face was creased with wrinkles caused by many hours working in the sunlight.

"Ah, *allô, allô! Oui, oui*, our good customers. *Mais oui,* we have your order all ready, but you mustn't just run off. Ah, *non*! It is an honor that you come to see us twice in just a few weeks. You must dine with us. No, no, I insist!" she said, as we started to demur.

The amount of champagne we were to transport daunted us somewhat, but we emptied the cases and started tucking the loose bottles in the back of the small Renault until the chassis sat low over the wheels. After we had finished loading, she led us into a large farmhouse. The aroma of homemade bread on the sideboard and coq au vin bubbling on the stove of the large kitchen put any further protestations to rest.

"But first, we must choose some champagne to drink with our meal. Come, come!"

We followed her through a series of buildings that housed the wine-making operation. A bottling machine stood in one area next to a corking machine that stoppered and foiled each bottle. Throughout the length of the building, thousands of bottles of champagne lay in racks, tipped neck down. As she explained the champagne-making process and the differences within the vintages, she moved down the racks, expertly giving each bottle a deft turn. This, she said, moved the sediment down into the neck, where it could be drawn off before corking.

"Ah, you must try this," she said, pulling bottles from the labeled shelves. "Yes, and this—and this—"

Her substantial lunch was no match for her potent wines. At her insistence we sampled everything, and when we finally waved good-bye to Madame Bonheur, we were quite intoxicated.

Rob, buried in champagne bottles in the back of the Renault, promptly fell into an alcohol-induced sleep replete with heavy snores. From the passenger seat, I tried to keep the skipper awake as he drove. Skipper John had a huge tolerance for alcohol, but even so, it was by the grace of God (and the lack of French police) that we made it to Paris unscathed. I was beginning to breathe easier as we approached the Champs Élysées.

At one end of the famous boulevard stands the Arc de Triomphe, in the center of what we English would call a huge roundabout. Six lanes of traffic fed by twelve avenues circumnavigate the arch, and the French drivers give way to the left, paying no attention at all to what is happening on their right sides. It was nearly six in the evening, and rush hour traffic was in full swing as we pulled up, ready to join the melee.

Suddenly John unbuckled his seat belt and opened the door. "I'm not driving," he announced. "Chris, you take it from here." He got out of the car, to the immediate blaring of horns behind us, and crawled into the back seat, waking the chef up.

"But—but—but—" I started to stammer. I'd never driven on the Continent, where one drives on the right-hand side of the road, as they do in America. I'd never driven a left-hand drive automobile. But my words were drowned out in the din of the impatient horns. So, taking a deep breath, I moved over and gingerly put the car into gear.

My companions obviously didn't share my fear. The skipper had already passed out while the chef, now awake but still drunk, was hanging out the back of the car, yelling *"Salut, ça va?!"*—the only French phrase he knew—at the other drivers.

"Just negotiate the roundabout," I told myself, as I slowly crept into traffic. Everything was backwards. I had to change gear with the wrong hand, and there was a crush of cars all around me, and there was so much weight in the back of the car that a sneeze would affect the steering. My hands were shaking, but I was now stone-cold sober.

"First—that's right, now second—good, you're going to do it, careful now, Christopher," I prattled to myself as we made what seemed to be an excruciatingly long way down the Champs Élysées to the Place de la Concorde and into the Touring Club. When I parked the car and got out, my weak knees owed nothing to alcohol.

Gary met us as we stumbled up the dock. "Pissed again, are we?" he started to laugh. I threw the keys at him.

"We picked it up. You can unload it. I'm going to bed."

Thereafter I confined my vineyard sampling to small tastes, as such visits occurred with some regularity. When no guests were expected on board for a few days, we were sent out to purchase wines for the cellar. As it was my job to recommend and pour all wines on board (not to mention being the only one of the crew who spoke even a smattering of schoolboy French), I was allowed to accompany the chef and skipper on these excursions, which took us to various vineyards throughout France. The result of my time spent in the wine regions of France has been useful to me since, though I must admit it has prejudiced me toward French red wine.

During our stay in Paris, I spent most of my free hours wandering the streets of the city, sampling burgundies and bordeaux, reading French cookbooks, trying the food in both the small bistros and the larger restaurants. In the early, foggy mornings, the fragrance of butter croissants, and the chicken and veal stocks being made for the day's soups and sauce bases would waft over the small back streets off the Rue de la Paix. When I could, I tagged along with Rob when he did the food shopping, marveling in the difference between English and French shops. Most impressive to me were the displays in the cases at the *boucheries*. My Co-Op training had taught me to recognize the cuts of meat, but never had I seen them more beautifully presented. On large serving platters, each steak or chop, cut precisely the same size, was tied with string and girdled with a feather-light slice of fat. Coiled sausages were plump to the point of bursting, and their ruddy color wasn't due to the pink fluorescent lights found back home. Unlike English shops, where meat sat indifferently on plastic plates with rubbery parsley, these displays were adorned with masses of scrubbed fresh vegetables and set off by an appropriate bottle of wine. And the breads! Having been brought up on hard rolls and Mother's Pride sliced white bread, I was amazed by the variety of shapes, sizes, and textures of the fare in the windows—floury rounds of shepherd's bread, crusty golden baguettes, plump dark loaves, and chewy whole-grain buns.

## A Short Lesson in Wines

In the households of long ago, not only did the butler select the right wines for the food chosen by the lady of the house and her cook, he was responsible for the actual racking, doctoring, and bottling of it, as well as the upkeep of the cellar book. These oenological functions were usually performed early in the morning, before the rest of the household was up and about. Prior to the meal, he decanted the sherry, port, and red wine, chilled champagne and white wine, and tasted the wine before it was served to ensure that it was acceptable. From newspaper reports and servants' manuals of the period, it seems that insobriety was a common failing among butlers, and probably one of the reasons why masters in the nineteenth century began to take more of an interest in the contents of their cellars.

*Wine Bottling Sizes*

| | |
|---|---|
| Split | ¼ bottle; 187 ml.; 6 to 6.5 oz. |
| "Pint" or half | ½ bottle; 375 ml.; 11 to 13 oz. |
| Bottle | 750 ml.; 24 to 26 oz. |
| Magnum | 2 bottles; 52 oz. |
| Marie-jeanne | 3 bottles; 78 oz. |
| Jeroboam or double magnum | 4 bottles; 104 oz. |
| Tappit-hen | 128 oz. (1 gal.) |
| Rehoboam | 6 bottles; 156 oz. (1.22 gal.) |
| Imperial | 8 bottles; 208 oz. (1.625 gal.) |
| Methuselah | also 8 bottles; a different shape than Imperial |
| Salmanazar | 12 bottles; 312 oz. (2.44 gal.) |
| Balthazar | 16 bottles; 416 oz. (3.3 gal.) |
| Nebuchadnezar | 20 bottles; 520 oz. (4.07 gal.) |
| Demijohn | 627.2 oz. (4.9 gal.) |

Wine is best stored horizontally in a clean, dark, dry place. Ideally it should be kept at approximately fifty-four degrees Fahrenheit, with no substantial changes in temperature or movement. But while it is better to keep wine cooler than the ideal rather than warmer, *consistency* of

*(continued on next page)*

*(continued from previous page)*
temperature is the most important factor in wine storage.

*Decanting.* An older wine, particularly a red wine, may contain sediment. Take the bottle from the cellar the day before serving and stand it upright; most of the sediment will settle to the bottom. To decant, clean the bottle with a damp cloth, uncork, and then slowly pour contents into a decanter, using a light or candle placed behind the bottle. This allows you to see the sediment approaching the neck. If lack of notice or forethought prevents you from standing the bottle upright for twenty-four hours, the next best thing is to remove the cork as gently as possible while holding the bottle at a forty-five degree angle. Double two layers of cheesecloth over the neck of the decanter. Gradually bringing the bottle to a horizontal position, pour the wine *very slowly* through the cheesecloth, using a candle to forewarn the approach of sediment. Leave the last small portion of the wine in the bottle if the sediment is very heavy; it is better to have ninety percent of clear wine than one hundred percent of murky, gritty wine. (Watch the specialty beers as well —some have yeast fermented in the bottle, which appears as white lumps.)

In quieter moments on the boat, the chef taught me to develop menus complemented by various wines, and to create the sauces that graced the fine meats, which I practiced by volunteering to cook for the crew on his day off. The exquisite ingredients available made the lessons an exhilarating experience.

I had been with the *Rainbow* nearly three months before I finally met her owner.

"The boss is on his way," the skipper informed me one morning. "We're heading out this evening."

"Oh? Where are we going?"

"Don't know yet. Probably over to the Channel Islands. He usually brings the family on the trip out of Paris, but this time he's on his own, so it could be anywhere."

Around lunchtime, a shiny grey Rolls Royce Corniche pulled up within sight of the boat. The man who emerged was formidable in appearance. Standing nearly six feet tall, with a long, angular face etched deeply by the sun, Mr. Griffith was not so much an attractive man as a striking one. Only the shock of grey in his thick brown hair betrayed his sixty-plus years.

As he came aboard, the captain introduced me. For a long moment Mr. Griffith looked over his thick, black-rimmed glasses, his blue eyes seeming like headlights that could illuminate my soul. He could be a Queen's Counsel lawyer, I thought—that is, until he opened his mouth. His muddy Midlands accent was genial.

"Hullo, Christopher. Glad to have you aboard," he said, shaking my hand. His face broke into a smile as he looked down the length of the deck. "Right, lods, let's go. I've a mind to head for Guernsey, eh?" And off we went.

I was with the *Rainbow* three summer seasons. Each year we'd begin the period with the Paris trip, then Mr. Griffith would fly over from England and we'd take him, and sometimes his family, down the Seine, and then perhaps to the Channel Islands, or Deauville, or Sark for a while. There we'd stay a week or two after he and his family had flown home until we got a call to motor off to another port, where various guests would join us.

His wife, busy with the children and other interests, was not a sailor; therefore, we rarely saw her. Sometimes, however, we did see Noëlle, Mr. Griffith's girlfriend, and once in a great while, her visits would overlap with those of his children, two spoiled young daughters who delighted in stirring up trouble. On those (thankfully) rare occasions, he wanted the kids to sleep forward in the crew's quarters, rather than the guest stateroom, so that he could entertain Noëlle in unmuffled delight.

Mr. Griffith primarily, however, came aboard alone, and

when he did he was around all the time—getting a tan, having endless drinks, reading, talking and joking with the crew, or just relaxing. Because most of the time he came sailing after he and his wife had had a fight, we had very little notice of his arrival. As the boat was always maintained in readiness for such an occurrence, this was not too much of a concern for us; rather, it was always an adventure. Jovial and down-to-earth, Mr. Griffith was in many ways a big kid who enjoyed his toys, and the Rolls and the *Rainbow* were his two favorites. We'd get a call from him: "Right, lods; I'm cooming down to th' boot," and within a few hours his chauffeur would pull up in the Rolls. We'd fire up the engines and head for ports on the south coast of England, the Channel Islands, or the Brittany coast.

By all accounts he was an astute businessman who worked very hard and relished the wheeling and dealing that was part of his business. But when he was on board, he was there to play, and occasionally he wanted us to play too, which was highly unusual in the trade. But then, Mr. Griffith was a singular employer.

Once, we had been moored in Weymouth, on England's south coast, for a couple of weeks. It was late morning and we were in the pub opposite the mooring, when out of nowhere our boss walked in, his mousy-brown hair windblown. Caught off guard, we stumbled to our feet and attempted to look presentable, but he waved us back in our seats and ordered himself a drink.

"Hullo, lods. Drove up, knew you'd be in the pub. The wife has declared war on me, and I fancy getting away. Cowes, maybe." Downing his drink in a single gulp, he dropped some money on the bar and stood up. "Are you ready? Right, then; let's go."

He'd clearly had a few on the way down, and we too had been drinking for a few hours and were fairly inebriated. Nevertheless, we went aboard the *Rainbow,* called the Coast Guard for clearance, and set off. Mr. Griffith retired to his cabin for a nap, while the skipper, who was far too drunk to sail, pulled the boat out of the harbor. Passing the outer seawall, I was seasick for the first time in my life, but felt a lot better than the rest of the crew, so I volunteered to take the helm to Cowes.

"You're halfway sober; you'll do," the skipper agreed.

Cowes is the largest port on the Isle of Wight, a small island off the southern coast of England, measuring just twenty-three miles long by eleven miles wide. Because of the *Rainbow's* size we radioed ahead, requesting a berth large enough to hold us. As we entered the harbor at about half-past two in the afternoon, the skipper reappeared, sober now, to take over the wheel, just as Mr. Griffith emerged from his stateroom.

"Right, lods," he said, "let's go get summat to eat."

The crew needed no second invitation. We tied up and locked the *Rainbow* with alacrity, and together we walked up to a hotel in which we'd often had a drink.

The only occupant of the lounge was a solitary barkeep. "Sorry," he said. "We're just closing."

"But we've only just docked, and we're hungry," Mr. Griffith said. "Might I speak to the manager?"

Unfortunately this individual, when summoned, also proved unhelpful. "I'm sorry sir, but the chef is just leaving."

"Please ask him if he'd come speak with us."

After a moment or two, the chef appeared, wearing only his vest with his houndstooth chef's trousers. Mr. Griffith peeled a number of twenty pound notes from his money clip and put them down in front of the man.

"Will that be enough to keep the restaurant open?"

The chef's eyes bulged, and when he spoke, it was with a stammer. "S-s-sure. What can I do for you?"

Ah, life in a small town. Before we had finished our meal of roast pork and mashed potatoes, word had got round to the locals that some rich man had paid the chef a week's wages to stay open. Consequently, the saloon bar, which had reopened for evening business, was packed when we came in. And they weren't disappointed. Mr. Griffith bought a continual round of drinks for all.

Around ten o'clock, unable to feel my face, I was edging

my way through the crowd to the door when I saw an odd sight. Mr. Griffith was handing a beer to someone laying on the floor near his feet. Looking closer, I saw that it was Rob, who had passed out and slithered under the barstool. "Right, lod," Mr. Griffith was saying, as he set the beer down on Rob's chest, "If you want to drink laying down, that's okay."

Stealing away, I went to bed and had no idea when the rest of the boat's occupants rolled in. But at half-past four in the morning I heard someone moving around upstairs. Thinking that the boss was perhaps feeling the effects of his night out, I donned my dressing gown and crept upstairs to investigate, following the sounds to the galley.

It was Mr. Griffith all right, but he didn't seem to be the worse for his drinking; he was rummaging through the cupboards looking for something to eat. In spite of the informality of his attitude to me and the rest of the crew, I was conscious of not being properly attired, so I slipped away, had a quick shave, and dressed hastily in my uniform. Then I ran back upstairs to the galley, to find him cooking bacon.

"Oh, sir, please let me do that. I'll make you breakfast."

"Good morning, Christopher!" He greeted me with more energy than I could imagine, given the hour and the previous evening's antics. "No, no, its not my breakfast, lod, it's our breakfast. Go and get everyone up. No, you go on," he said, shrugging off my protest.

When the crew, in various states of dishabille, staggered up to the galley, they stopped short in amazement. Five bottles of Mouton Cadet red wine were lined up along the marble bar. To the right of each stood a wineglass, and in front, four bacon sandwiches were piled on each of five monogrammed china plates.

"Come on, lods, eat up. We've got a big day ahead of us. Best get it off to a good start!"

# 3

# Moored in the Mediterranean

If life as a "yachtie" was somewhat glamorous, it was offset by its instability. Not only was the work highly seasonal, but if a boat was sold—and boats were sold often in the late 1970's and early 1980's—the new owner almost always had his own crew. Thus it was that when a reversal of fortune in his company forced Mr. Griffith to sell the *Rainbow* to someone else, all of us were laid off.

The last trip we'd taken with Mr. Griffith was to Majorca, an island off the coast of Spain. As we weren't due back in London again for several weeks, our cruise homeward had been leisurely and full of detours, sailing into or past many Mediterranean ports, including Oran, Marseilles, and Barcelona. One day we cruised past the harbors of the Côte d'Azur in the south of France. Although we didn't moor, the view of the occupants of those marinas in the early morning sun was enough to stop me dead in the water.

"Bloody hell," I breathed.

Until that time, in my experience the *Rainbow* had always been the biggest boat in any harbor we'd ever docked. But even from a distance, the shimmery white yachts that were moored in the marina at Monte Carlo made me feel our trim eighty-five-foot beauty was a poor relation.

"That's where the big money is," I said in awe. "That's where I'm going."

And so it was that, when I was subsequently laid off, I looked for a way to get to the south of France in time for the yachting season. When I found a temporary job crewing a barge across the English Channel and down the canals of France to Provence, I was elated. But my elation turned to dismay when the trip was unexpectedly delayed midway, with the result that by the time I made it to Cannes, most of the crews had already been hired for the season.

Strung along the Côte d'Azur like a necklace of glittering jewels, the resort towns that include St. Tropez, Cannes, Nice, and Monte Carlo are the domain of the very wealthy. Yet even against the backdrop of old-world elegance of this legendary playground of the rich and royal, nothing was more spectacular than the yachts. And no one is as rich as those who own them. Here was pure, unadulterated disposable income—complete homes, built to float. The largest vessels ranged from 120 to 220 feet long. Often they were commissioned from yacht builders and heavily customized. It was not unusual to spend twenty million dollars building a Feadship or a Benetti, then spend an additional seven million dollars to furnish it. These magnificent floating palaces might have marble fireplaces, staircases, and floors, walls made of rare woods, crystal chandeliers, or hand-painted murals. The bedrooms—they were so different from what one pictures a sleeping berth to be that "stateroom" hardly applies—were often as big as those found on land; and adjacent bathrooms featured such luxuries as marble walls and pounded nickel sinks. Outside, there might be a Jacuzzi on deck—some even had small swimming pools—and, in addition to a motorboat and assorted toys such as Jet Skis, they often had helipads on the top deck for immediate excursions elsewhere. In the many harbors between Hyéres and Menton, there were hundreds of such mega-yachts, secured superciliously in their moorings opposite the more ordinary motorboats. The sight of so much floating real estate changes the way one looks at a marina forever.

But life is impossibly expensive on the Côte d'Azur for the less-than-well-to-do. I wasn't known in the south of France; my "yachtie" connections were all in England and Paris. Each day I walked back and forth between the ports on either side of Cannes looking for work, hitchhiking to the others if I could, buying cigarettes in lieu of food because they alleviated the hunger somewhat. Lined up in Port Canto at Cannes and Port Vauban at Antibes, the lazy elegance of the yachts mocked the common man who only worked there. Over and over I made the circuit, calling, "Do you have any jobs?" as I rapped on their sterns. With luck, I would get a day job cleaning or scrubbing barnacles, varnishing the rails, polishing the brightwork—whatever was needed.

A man named Jacob, for whom I'd done some day work, was the skipper on the *Pride of Bethlehem.* Often as I made my rounds he'd hail me.

"Hey, Chris! Found anything?"

"Not yet."

"Hey, I was just going for a sandwich. Come join me."

I was sure he'd already eaten, and that he forced that sandwich down in order to buy me one, which, if I hadn't found a day job, was my only meal of the day. I blessed him silently.

In spite of my best efforts to find a job, it wasn't long before my money ran out. I was down to my last seven francs when I faced the decision to give it up. Not able to afford even a cheap hotel, I had spent two nights sleeping on the beach at Cannes, my impoverished presence a bizarre contrast to the line of glittering hotels on the Croisette behind me, and the procession of obscene opulence in the Vieux Port before me. I made a deal with myself—if I didn't find work that day, I would buy one last packet of cigarettes and start hitchhiking home.

It was nearly 3:00 in the afternoon when I made my way back from Antibes, tired, hungry, and discouraged, to find Jacob standing on the deck of his boat.

"Where have you been?" he shouted to me, waving his arms wildly. "I've got a job for you!"

Exhausted and unbelieving, I looked at him, speechless, as he rattled on. "I know this man Jacques, he's a skipper on the *Temptation,* and I told him about you. They're in the Vieux Port. Go see him, quick!"

I reached the berth of *Temptation* about 3:45, where a skinny older man with a narrow chest and sloping shoulders answered my hello. He wore a dirty T-shirt and his dark hair was in serious need of a cut and, much to my surprise, he introduced himself as the man I'd come to see. The only other crew member, Georges the engineer, was somewhat neater in appearance.

Jacques explained that the *Temptation* was owned by a French video producer whom the crew hadn't seen since last season. That morning, with no warning, he had turned up with instructions to get everything ready; he wanted a party that night. As I was shown to the smallest crew's quarters I had ever occupied, Jacques said, almost casually, "Did you say you can cook?"

"Yes, sir."

"Good. We'll need a hot and cold buffet for seventy-five people by eight o'clock."

I looked at my watch. Less than four hours away! Hurriedly dropping my duffel bags in the none-too-clean berth, I headed for the galley, to receive yet another shock.

It was apparent to me that, unlike any other boat I had ever been on, the *Temptation*'s crew did nothing in the way of cleaning and maintenance during the off-season when the owners weren't expected. The small galley was coated in dust and grime; only the top of the counters was clean. From the doorway I could see dirty fingerprints on cupboard doors, and there were footprints in the grease on the floor. Most alarmingly, there was no food aboard. I questioned the skipper.

"That's all right; we've hired a stewardess for the night from another boat. She's bringing the food. Her name's Cassie, and she should be along any moment."

Fighting a rising sense of panic, I assessed what staples were on hand (very few) and started cleaning the galley. I had it presentable by five o'clock, when Cassie arrived in her car. "Here's stuff. Make stuff," Jacques told me, as the three of them shuffled in the bags of provisions.

The food seemed to be bought at random. As I unloaded the bags, I found a whole cooked salmon, assorted shellfish—prawns, crabs, languistino—in all sizes, filets of swordfish, canned Polish ham, a whole sirloin, a shoulder of lamb, smoked breast of turkey, a few pounds of canned beans, and an assortment of vegetables. In one bag I came across something I'd never seen before—couscous. Bloody hell, what do you serve *that* with? I wondered.

Using the beans as a starting point, I made a big tureen of soup, and let it simmer on the back burner while I cleaned the shellfish. I made crepes, then prepared the shellfish in a cream sauce on the stove, and put the swordfish in a baking dish with white wine and lemon juice. I sliced up some of the many baguettes and toasted them, then started creating hors d'oeuvres out of whatever was at hand—some tiny shrimp, a sliver of avocado, a slice of cherry tomato, a dollop of curried mayonnaise.

I had no time to roast the lamb, which was too fatty for presentation anyway, so I cut it all off the bone and made a lamb curry with it. As the couscous looked like rice, I thought maybe curry would go with it, so I served them in adjacent pans in the same chafing dish. In another chafing dish I assembled the seafood crepes; a warming dish displayed slices of sirloin steak cooked rare and drizzled with a canned béarnaise sauce and capers.

The poached salmon was served on a bed of lettuce accented with wheels of lemon and crowned tomatoes, and accompanied by a dill sauce. Platters of sliced cold ham and turkey were rolled and displayed with an assortment of rolls and chutneys, mustards, and mayonnaise. The remaining baguettes I stood in an old ceramic pot, washed and draped with napkins, which added height to the table. Fortunately I

### Resuscitating a Soufflé (or, How to Make Something Wonderful Out of a Disaster)

Back in the 1950's and 1960's there was a running joke about the difficulty of making a soufflé. The delicate concoction that was so prone to falling seemed to be a housewife's worst nightmare. The scene: "What's for dinner, dear?" the bumbling husband asks. Before the frantic wife can stop him, he opens the oven door, causing ruin to the soufflé designed for his boss, who is Coming to Dinner.

Unfortunately many people forego the making of soufflés to this day because they believe them to be temperamental, fussy desserts (and main courses). But nothing could be further from the truth. Given the proper tools—a soufflé dish and a good mixer—soufflés are fairly simple, and much less time-consuming than one would think. Certainly their preparation is far quicker than that of an iced cake, even one made with a boxed mix. Because soufflés—like many gateaux, Baked Alaskas, and flambéed fruit—are as much a showpiece as a sweet ending to a meal, they are customarily brought to the table whole, to much oohing and ahhing, and served there. Unless you're a professional gourmet cook and your dinner guests include other gourmet cooks, it doesn't matter if your soufflé has risen a little more on one side than another. It still looks marvelous, and tastes even better.

The only time I was unhappy enough with a soufflé to refuse to present it "as is," the problem had nothing to do with an oven door slamming or heavy tread in the kitchen; it was due to my overuse of fresh juice in the batter. Because the juice was highly acidic, it curdled my batter somewhat so that it refused to rise, light and airy, in the dish. This is how I covered my tracks.

The soufflé in question was lemon. I took from the freezer a bag of frozen unsweetened raspberries, spread

*(continued on next page)*

*(continued from previous page)*
them in a single layer on a plate, and microwaved them one minute in order to thaw them somewhat. Then I took half of the berries, puréed them in the blender, and combined the paste in the top of a double-boiler with half a cup of sugar, the same amount of jam from the refrigerator (in this case, it happened to be strawberry), and a tablespoon of cornstarch. I cooked the mixture, stirring, over boiling water until it was thickened, then set the pan in iced water to cool it a bit. Using large wine glasses, I layered soufflé, sauce, and whole berries, repeating twice and ending with whole berries, and served the result as a parfait. The contrast between the sweet raspberries and the tart lemon was wonderful, as was the color, and the guests never knew that they weren't being served the dessert I'd planned in the first place!

didn't have to make desserts, as they had bought an assortment of bakery cakes and tarts.

I could hear guests starting to arrive as I prepared to transfer the soup to its serving tureen. But when I tasted it, to my dismay I found it bland. In a desperate attempt to give it some flavor, I pulled spices at random from the cupboard and added lots of everything. Then I tasted it again. It nearly blew the roof off my mouth.

Well, too late now. Placing the tureen on the buffet table, I added a little sign to the front that said "HOT!"

As the party got underway, I positioned myself behind the buffet table and served the guests. What Jacques hadn't told me was that the owner, and the majority of the guests, were French Moroccan. I didn't know if they would even like this sort of food.

One of the principal guests, a large, dark man with a bulbous red nose and heavy, dark eyebrows, made a beeline for my soup.

"The soup is quite spicy, sir," I said.

"That eez okay. Me, I like spicy foods," the gentleman replied.

I watched him anxiously when he sat down and started to eat. As he spooned the spicy liquid into his mouth, I could see the sweat break out on his brow. His cheeks and large nose grew redder, and his thick eyebrows knitted until there was a single dark black line over his eyes. Suddenly he jumped up and approached the buffet table where I stood, the bowl in his hands.

"Thiz eez *fabulous*!" he said. And he handed me his bowl for seconds.

In spite of the success of the party, I was unhappy working on the *Temptation*. I found the slovenly condition of the boat as I'd first seen it to be a reflection of the attitude of the crew. But one bright spot in the matter was that I'd met Cassie. She and her husband worked on the *Serendipity*, a far grander (and better maintained) boat than the *Temptation*. When, several weeks later, a steward position became available on *Serendipity*, she recommended me, and I literally jumped ship. Years later, I was able to return the favor.

I was working on *Serendipity* one summer when we had an American guest on board named Mr. Reynolds. Mr. Reynolds was considerably younger than his hosts, with a cheerful thatch of red hair and laughing eyes. He was traveling alone and, being a friendly sort, he struck up an acquaintance with me and a couple of the lads on the boat.

We were docked in Alcudia, and just around the bend of the shore the cliffs formed a quiet, serene horseshoe bathing beach. Although beautiful to look at, the rocks that studded this tiny cove made it accessible only by motorboat. One morning, when Mr. Reynolds was at a loss for something to do, we suggested making him a picnic lunch and running him over to the beach in the motorboat. He brightened immediately and requested some sandwiches and beer, which we prepared and packed while he went off to change.

When we picked him up that afternoon, he seemed rested and cheered. But with a comical face, he related that his fellow bathers on the beach had been quite unfriendly.

"What a bunch of snobs," he laughed. "You should have

## Presentation Technique: Displaying the Cork With an Open Wine Bottle

With the bottle upright and its label facing you, make a cut in the foil on top of the bottle with a sharp knife, starting at point A and cutting clockwise to point B. Leave about ¼" uncut. (Note this position is to the right of the label as you face it.) Moving down the neck of the bottle to the top of the lip, from the same relative starting point A, make another cut around the bottle, ending at point B and again leaving ¼" of foil uncut.

Fold both the ring and the top circle back at the uncut "hinge." Remove the cork.

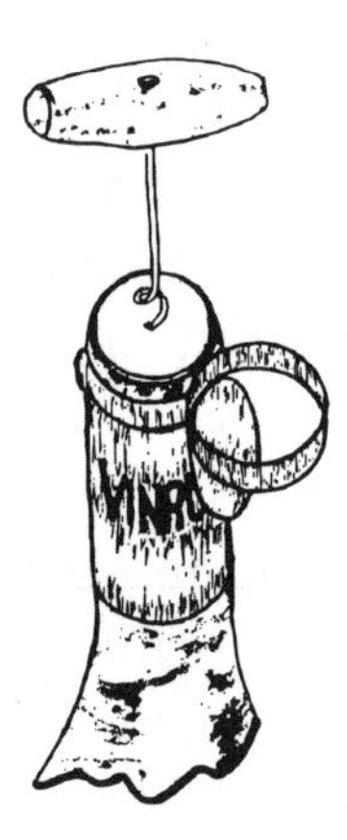

Insert the cork into the ring and fold the foil excess tightly against the cork to hold it in place.

When you pour, the cork should be on the top of the bottle and the label should be facing the recipient.

seen their noses go up at lunchtime when I opened my picnic basket and got out my sandwiches. They, you see, had this entire spread laid out with salads and desserts and little plastic wineglasses. I kinda felt like I'd gone to a party and hadn't gotten the dress code right. I sure didn't cut any ice with them."

Although he spoke lightly, the incident had obviously bothered him. So before dinner, I spoke to the chef and we came up with a plan.

"Don't you worry about those people on the beach, sir," I told him as I served him dinner that evening. "Tomorrow, you go back to that beach. I assure you that they'll be the ones to feel under-dressed."

In spite of his curiosity, we wouldn't tell him our scheme, and the next morning we dropped him at the beach in the motorboat at 9:00 A.M. We could see a handful of other parties lounging under umbrellas scattered over the sand.

"And what time would you be requiring lunch, sir?" I asked, making sure my voice carried on the wind.

"Oh, noon would be fine," Mr. Reynolds said in some surprise. I bowed slightly, giving him a wink. He smiled as we pulled the boat back offshore and set up his towel and beach chair.

At seven minutes to noon, with the large yacht moored as close to the beach as we dared, our motorboat putted around the rocks into the cove. Sonny, the deckhand, was at the tiller, and I stood in the prow, a folded tablecloth over my arm and a basket in my hand. I wore a short white tuxedo coat, a bowtie, and white trousers.

All eyes were upon us as we neared the shore. I kept my balance as Sonny grounded the boat and we both stepped out, he running ahead to set up a folding table and chair next to Mr. Reynolds. I covered the table with a thick white damask cloth, then from the basket, I set a full table complete with silver, a small vase of flowers, and *Serendipity*'s customized Royal Doulton china.

Mr. Reynolds' pale eyebrows disappeared into his red hair. With an effort he kept a straight face as he took his place at the table.

"I hope you don't mind, sir, but I took the liberty of choosing your wine. Will '61 Chateau Mouton-Rothschild Pauillac be to your liking?" I said clearly. It really wasn't a choice;

unbeknownst to the incredulous audience, that was the only vintage we had on board.

"Oh, that will be fine." Mr. Reynolds was starting to enjoy the game and, like mine, his voice was pitched to carry.

Sonny returned to the boat and brought me a large hamper, then reboarded the boat and motored off. I brought forth the promised wine, opened it with a flourish, presented the cork for his approval, and at his nod, poured the first glass of wine. As he sipped, I laid before him an appetizer of rolled smoked salmon with horseradish and hot brown bread and butter.

"Cracked pepper, sir?"

"Please."

I stood behind him and slightly to his right, as, stifling giggles, he began to eat. Midway through the chilled soup course, I removed a walkie-talkie from my belt and spoke into it.

"Mr. Reynolds will have the main course now."

"Straightaway," the chef's voice crackled over the receiver, and a few minutes later Sonny reappeared in the motorboat with a new hamper.

In this manner we served him a four course meal, concluding with a miniature Baked Alaska (flambéed) for dessert. During the whole of the meal there wasn't a sound from the other bathers around us.

Much later we picked up Mr. Reynolds to return him to the boat. As we rounded the bend from the cove, he gave way to the laughter he'd suppressed since lunch.

"That was the best thing I've ever seen," he said, wiping tears from his eyes. "As long as I live, I don't think I'll forget the sight of you steaming in with that platter in your hands.

"And you know," he winked, "I've been invited to dinner in town tonight with one Michele C—, the daughter of a baron. Do you think you could arrange for late night drinks on board?"

# 4

# Private Service

"I'm going to sell the house," my father announced.

"You're what?" I asked, plugging my finger deeper into my ear. The pub noise grew to a crescendo around me as the darts teams neared the end of their game.

"I'm going to sell the house," he repeated. "It's too much to keep up, and I can't manage it on my pension. I'll get a council flat and live off the remaining cash from the sale."

This was not good news. I was ringing from the Bar des Anglais, my favorite English pub in Monte Carlo, where the crews of the yachts enjoyed their off-hours. The familiar sights and sounds evoked a wave of homesickness. Darlene, the barmaid, handed me another pint as I made up my mind.

"Dad, don't sell the house. My only roots to anywhere are in that house, and if you sell it, I'll have nowhere to come home to. Listen, I'll buy it off you and take care of your bills. The house will be my savings account for the future."

I hung up with a headache that owed nothing to the six pints of Bass shandy I'd had so far. Now I needed a real job.

At the time, I was working on the *Enigma,* a 125-foot yacht that had once been the best cruising charter boat in the business. Now, however, she seemed to be permanently moored in San Remo. This was because her owner, Sir Graham Black, had acquired a new bride, a pretty twenty-five-year-old former model whom he didn't trust. A doddering old goat, Sir Graham was so worried about his wife having an affair that he timed everything she did. If she was getting her hair done, for example, he'd allow her a certain amount of time to be gone, and then he expected her back. Needless to say, his concern didn't allow him much time to sail, so the *Enigma* was on the market. Of course, when the yacht was sold, chances were I'd be out of a job anyway. But as boats were selling slowly in those days, none of the *Enigma*'s crew was particularly active in seeking other employment.

But with a mortgage and a dependent, I couldn't afford to be a steward anymore.

"Problem, luv?" asked Darlene, noting my preoccupation.

"I need a landside job—a steady one," I told her. "Commitments back home."

No matter where in the world you go, an English-style pub seems to attract expatriates as staff. The pub is an integral part of English life, and English publicans are usually a wealth of information, a sort of living notice board. Darlene thought for a moment, then her face brightened. "Do you know Faith, the stewardess on *Sundial*?"

*Sundial* was a private yacht owned by an ex-Russian prince who wasn't around much. I had to admit that, although I had met a few of the crew, the stewardess had escaped my notice.

"Well, she was telling me about her brother-in-law, who's a retired butler. Some Lord or Lady needs a butler right now, and is trying to get him to come and work there again. He really doesn't want the job. Why don't you do that?"

"A butler? Like Jeeves?" I perked up. "What exactly does a butler do, in real life?"

"I don't know, exactly. But I expect it's a bit like what you're doing on the boat—stewarding, I mean. Serve the people, say 'yes, sir, yes madame'—that sort of thing. Why don't you talk to Faith about it?"

I looked up Faith aboard *Sundial* straightaway and explained my predicament. The following day found me having tea in the *Sundial*'s crew's mess with Faith and her brother-in-law, William.

William was English, short and very thin, with a big nose and the yellow pallor of a lifetime smoker. His first words gave me a shock; I expected anyone who made their living as a butler to have an upper-crust, BBC-type accent, but William was very much a Cockney.

"It's like this, mate," he said, brushing straggly Bryl-creemed hair from his red-rimmed weepy eyes. "I've worked for Lady Welsh before, and she's all right, as they go. But I don't really need the job, and to tell you the truth, I daren't take a job that needs me to live in." And he told a curious story.

While William had worked as an under-butler for Lady Welsh as a young man, he had subsequently taken a job with a Turkish pasha for whom he had worked much of his adult life. The pasha had a large house in Cannes. As butlers are usually required to live in, he and his wife, Iris, were housed in a little cottage on the grounds of the estate. Iris wasn't, strictly speaking, in the trade, but she had helped out on an "as-needed" basis.

In the past year, the Pasha had died, which put William out of a job. But at the reading of the will, he and Iris had a pleasant surprise—the Pasha had directed that in addition to a small pension, William and Iris were to continue to be allowed to live in the cottage, rent-free, for the rest of their lives. It was one of those rare bequests that most lifelong servants only dream of, and William was very grateful for his good fortune. Although Iris was younger, William was getting on in years, and he'd saved enough over his lifetime that with the pension and a rent-free cottage, he didn't need to work. But the Pasha had a son, who had inherited the rest of the estate and wanted to sell the house. Because it would be impossible to sell a property with a retired servant living in the cottage indefinitely, he wanted them to leave.

In the midst of all this, Lady Welsh had recently reappeared, and was desperate. She had begged William to come work for her again, telling him he could live in his own cottage if he preferred. But it was then September, and William knew that in April, Lady Welsh would go to her summer home in Switzerland and expect him to come with her. He also knew that if he left his cottage for any length of time, the Pasha's son would take it away, arguing that he obviously didn't need it as he was never there, etc. He'd evict William and sell the house.

William couldn't afford a court battle. He'd been in the South of France long enough to know that the rich control the Côte d'Azur, and that Money would win, every time. And besides, he didn't want the job. After I'd apprised him of my background and interest, he offered to pass my name along to Lady Welsh.

I asked him what a butler did, because I had no idea. "Basically, you're a glorified waiter," he told me. Silly me, I took him at his word.

William arranged for me to have an interview with Lady Welsh the next day at her villa in the exclusive neighborhood of St. Jean Cap Ferrat. I spent the remainder of the evening trying to learn something about my potential employer. All I could determine was that she was English, and that she had come by most of her wealth through one of her deceased husbands, whose family was a leading landowner in the United Kingdom.

Shortly after two in the afternoon the following day, dressed in my crested Rainbow blazer, I borrowed a car and followed William's directions to the Villa Bianco. Passing the tiny village that contained little else other than a few coffee bars and patisseries fronting a small harbor for yachts, I continued into the residential area, catching tantalizing glimpses of luxurious villas behind high stone walls. Cool, slightly salty breezes blew off the sea, but the temperature was balmy. As I was early, I parked the car and made my way along the public footpath that winds all around the edge of the peninsula of St. Jean Cap Ferrat in order to get my bearings.

All of the houses were on the land side of the footpath save one, which I later learned belonged to the English actor David Niven. Situated on a small cove facing Beaulieu, the estate I had come to visit was surrounded by a massive stone wall, behind which grew a thick hedge of mock orange, making it impossible to see the house or grounds from the footpath. A small door in the wall facing the sea stood opposite a hook-shaped stone jetty, which enclosed a rowboat. I could imagine the view over the bay from the house was magnificent.

Still a little in advance of my appointment, I returned to the front of the property and approached the entrance. From the road, a pair of pillars flanked slatted wooden gates that rose some eight feet high and were blank except for an iron ring. There was no gatehouse visible and no one to meet me. Surely, if I just walk in, an alarm will go off somewhere, I thought. With some trepidation, I turned the ring, which flipped up a lever inside, and opened the gates. No alarm sounded.

Grandness in boats I had become accustomed to; grandness in houses was something else altogether. My eyes widened as I gazed at the property before me.

A neatly kept gravel drive bisected a manicured lawn bordered with brightly flowering shrubs in shades of fuchsia, hot pink, and crimson. On the right hand side I could see a number of sweeping border gardens, each containing perennials and climbing roses in softer hues of salmon, shell pink, and lilac. Gnarled olive trees were shaped topiary-style; large clumps of dusty grey-green leaves had been sheared into balls that reminded me of the tails of Parisian poodles. Climbing tendrils of amethyst bougainvillea nearly obscured the trunks of the large palm trees that dotted the lawn, their fronds making a papery swishing sound as the light breeze played through them. The dark green of the cypresses that edged the property formed a frame round the scene. The drive wound down a slight incline, culminating in a grand circular portico, set off by a large fountain, at the entrance of the house.

As its name suggested, the Villa Bianco was a sprawling milky white Mediterranean estate with a sooty terracotta tile roof. It seemed more of a complex than a single house, with many angles emanating from a central structure. Numerous small, shuttered windows and wrought-iron balconies broke up the expanse of rough white stucco.

Suddenly, out of nowhere, a battalion of tiny Pekinese dogs appeared at my feet, yapping shrilly as they attempted to scale my legs. They were joined by a slightly more sedate Pointer that I viewed as more of a threat. Dogs? William hadn't mentioned anything about dogs, and I was allergic to them. Surrounded now, I was trying to remain calm and befriend the animals when a large woman in a bright, flowing caftan limped heavily around the hedge.

She was of medium height but very overweight, with fuzzy, blue-rinsed hair and pudgy hands peppered with liver spots. Skillful makeup couldn't hide the lines etched deep by age and sun, and I guessed her age—rightly, as it turned out—at around seventy. Small, deep-set eyes peered at me from a face embellished by otherwise large features—thin lips framed a wide mouth, accented by a wide, square jaw. Gnarled knuckles were crusted with rings and her large ears dripped jewels. When she spoke, her voice sounded like a man speaking in falsetto.

"Down!" she commanded, somehow drawing out the word into three syllables. Snuffling, the little dogs retreated behind her skirts, where they watched me warily through their protruding oversized eyes.

I was in the process of thanking her when she interrupted me.

"You're English, then?"

"Yes, madame, I am."

"Good. You'll start tomorrow."

I adjusted my tie and collar, checked my cuffs, and tugged ineffectively at the rather cheap-looking white jacket that Lady Welsh had issued me. Except for the jacket, my uniform was essentially the same as my steward's uniforms had been aboard the boats—white shirt, black trousers, socks, shoes, and tie during the day; a starched white dress shirt, bowtie, and white gloves at night.

### Carriage and Deportment

- Before leaving your private quarters for work, check to make sure hair is neat, fingernails are clean, shirt cuffs are immaculate, shoes are polished to a shine, jacket is brushed of all lint, and shoulders are free of dandruff, and show no signs of wear. Check these points regularly several times a day.
- Except for a wedding ring and a watch, wear no jewelry.
- Visit a barber regularly. Hair should be kept short and neat—above the ears and the collar. I once worked with an under-butler who had a serious cowlick, right in the middle of his head. If a good cut can't correct such a problem, gel your hair!
- A belt should be worn with black uniform trousers. A belt no wider than one inch with a small brass buckle is best.
- Proper tuxedo shirts do not have frills on the shirt fronts. Nor do they have blouson sleeves.
- French cuffs are fine for dinner service, but not for lunch.
- Shoes should always be very clean and polished. Have them heeled and soled before they show signs of wear.
- Wear only black socks with black shoes and trousers.
- During a long working day on your feet, get instant relief by putting on a fresh pair of socks. This feels great and works wonders.
- Always have a spare pair of clean white gloves.
- Stand tall in your uniform. Proper posture shows that you have pride in yourself and in your job.
- Take control of your gait; walk with poise and bearing. *Never run.* Not only is it undignified, it is unsafe.
- Speak only when spoken to, and think before you speak.
- Gauge your employer's mood before offering any comments other than greetings.

I didn't like the jacket at all. It was the type of inexpensively made service coat that is used by hotel staff, with white plastic buttons attached with cotter pins that can be taken off when laundering. I was too inexperienced to see it as a sign of the miserliness of my new employer.

With a last look at my hair, I reported to the kitchen for duty.

"Ah, Cristofaro. You are early yet; I am just starting our breakfast. Have a cup of coffee." Indicating the gleaming silver coffee urn on the counter opposite, Rudy invited me to sit down.

I had met the chef the previous evening when I had arrived with my small suitcases and been briefed on my duties. A second-generation Italian who had worked for Lady Welsh in the South of France for ten years, Rudy had immediately made me feel welcome in the large house. Grizzled and genial, he had a wide dark moustache that framed perfect teeth when he smiled, which was often. My West London accent had produced homesickness for his wife and three children who, I learned straightaway, lived in Croydon.

Already, Rudy had several pots and pans going on the stove, presumably for Lady Welsh's breakfast. It seemed rather a lot of food for just one woman, and I commented on this. Rudy laughed.

"Ah, there is not just her," he said. "You did not meet him, then? No, I expect not. He is sort of, how do you say, a nobody. But her ladyship does actually have a husband, called Mister Bristol. He is her fourth husband, and he is not titled; it is she who has all the money. And besides," he twinkled, indicating the cookware, "some of this is for the doggies."

"The *dogs*?" I goggled.

"Oh, yes. Yo Yo, Mitzi, Pippa, and Melisande—those are the Pekinese—have chopped cooked calves liver, or breast of chicken, or pork loin, or even fillet steak. Today I make them liver and chicken. Tabitha—that is the Pointer—she gets Pedigree Chum. It is time for their breakfast now. They should be here any minute."

On cue there was a generalized scuffling sound, punctuated by a paroxysm of high-pitched barking. The kitchen door banged open, and in burst the excited dogs. Behind them sailed a skinny, sour-looking woman with orange hair, carrying a tray with a stack of bowls on it. She stopped short on seeing me.

The bad dye job only accented her thinning hair, and her over-tweezed eyebrows gave her a perpetually surprised look. She looked at me suspiciously.

"Who eez theez?" Momentarily distracted, the dogs collected around my feet, barking.

Rudy spoke before I could. "This is Christopher, our new butler and chauffeur. Christopher, meet Isobel, personal maid to Lady Welsh. Isobel is the most senior member on the staff."

"How do y—"

When did *you* come?" she interrupted.

"Yesterday," I said, feeling somewhat uncomfortable under the malevolent glare she was leveling on me. Her thin, pinched nose tilted upward, as though she could smell something bad. I wondered if my deodorant had failed me.

"Why wasn't I notified?" she said, turning to Rudy. The implication, clearly, was why wasn't I consulted.

Rudy obviously was not afraid of her. His eyebrows rose in mock surprise. "Were you not off duty yesterday?"

She snorted. Ignoring me, she went to the stove, where she proceeded to dish the dogs' exalted breakfast into five individual porcelain bowls. Head held high, she swept out, followed by a small army of yapping furry pillows.

"Bloody hell, who was that?" I muttered to Rudy, digging into the plate of scrambled eggs he'd set before me.

"Ah, Isobel, pay no attention to her," he said, with a conspiratorial wink. "She is just a bitter old maid who hates everyone, especially the men. Not that anyone would have her. She is, how do you say, a bitch on wheels," he added parenthetically, disappearing into the butler's pantry. "She has been in service with Lady Welsh longer than anyone else on the staff, and she travels with them everywhere. She has arthritis, which you will see she makes the big production of when it is to her advantage. But do watch out for her. Me, I find it best just to stay out of her way as much as possible."

He emerged with a breakfast service of china I recognized as Royal Worcester, onto which he dished up a very English meal of soft-boiled eggs and toast soldiers with orange marmalade. A side dish of fresh melon and strawberries was the only concession to the fact that we were in the sunny South of France. From a small jar to one side of the stove, he plucked a few sprigs of blue wildflowers, which he used to garnish the plates. Finished, he took two polished silver covers down from above the stove and placed them over the dishes. "Isobel, she will be back in a moment to take the trays up to the mistress and master."

"Ah, that answers that question. I did wonder why I was told breakfast was the only meal I didn't serve."

"No, but you will want to do the newspaper to go up with the tray."

"The newspaper?" I was mystified.

He smiled. "You iron it."

"I iron it? Why?"

"I cannot *abide* those *annoying* creases," he said, mimicking Lady Welsh's falsetto voice rather accurately.

"Oh, crikey," I said, jumping up. Snatching the newspaper from the table, I hurried next door to the staff room where I'd seen the ironing board. How does one iron a newspaper? I wondered. On low heat, presumably? Should I use starch? What if the ink comes off on the iron? I could see I had a lot to learn to be a butler. I was definitely ringing William later about this one.

I had been at the iron for a few minutes when the door banged open and Isobel advanced on me, tray in hand. "Why eez zee paper not ready?" Seeing my stack of freshly ironed individual pages on the chair, she threw me a withering look. "You iron the whole section together, you stupeed. And then you fold it a leetle lengthwise, like theez." She demonstrated. Shaking her head at my ineptitude, she banged back out the door towards the stairs.

Well, I suppose one can't be liked by everyone.

# 5

# Journeyman Butler

Ironing the newspaper hadn't been mentioned in Lady Welsh's brief discussion of my duties the previous evening. She had decided, since I hadn't actual experience as a butler, that I would start as a sort of trainee butler-chauffeur and be paid accordingly. Once I had mastered my duties, I might expect a promotion. This sounded fair to me, as deep down I worried that even given my previous service background, I was somehow too inexperienced to be an actual butler. The newspaper incident underscored my concern. (Later, doing some research into the matter, I found the practice was originally done in order to set the ink so it wouldn't smudge the master's fingertips. Therefore, it *had* been necessary to iron each page, both sides. So there, Isobel, you stupeed!)

Primarily, I was to be responsible for setting and clearing at table, serving drinks and meals, and keeping the silver, china, and crystal in immaculate condition. In addition, I would drive Lady Welsh and Mr. Bristol when they went out and keep the cars in perfect running order. There were four: a pale green Rolls Royce Silver Spur, a Buick Electra station wagon, a Mercedes 450 SEL, and the staff car, a Mini Cooper Innocenti. I was given a monthly allowance of five hundred francs for petrol and incidentals, which I was to itemize as it would be scrupulously checked at the end of each month.

From the airy front hallway, double entry doors opened into the large sitting room where they were due at any moment for their morning coffee, the first meal I would serve to them. As I made one last check to ensure everything was in order, I marveled anew over the size of the Villa Bianco, the largest house I'd ever been in. I wondered if they actually used all of it, or whether, like a Dickens novel, there were rooms of furniture under white dust-sheets, old paintings stacked negligently against the wall.

Unlike cozy English homes, there wasn't a shred of wallpaper to be had in the house. All the walls were white, with a slight stucco texture that lent a bright, sunshiny effect and made the rooms seem even bigger. In the sitting room, this effect was augmented by a twelve-foot ceiling and the many windows that looked out over the gardens below. The windows were of plain design with simple wooden frames, and the draperies that surrounded them were unadorned. The few paintings that decorated the walls were muddy and nondescript.

A great deal of Spanish-style furniture sat about the room, the heavy, dark wood embellished with much hand carving and fretwork. Chairs and sofas, covered in a matching brightly colored floral pattern in shades of reds and blues, formed the only real color contrast in the room. Even the plants, spiky indoor palms, and sword-like Mother-in-law's tongue were angular, not bushy, and added to, rather than subtracted from, the stark, minimalistic look. I had somehow expected excesses of brocade, velvets, silks, and other richly textured materials, particularly in this, their most-used room, but it seemed I had a lot to learn about the wealthy. To my mind, while it was certainly a spacious, light room, it was not a particularly comfortable one.

From the hallway, a vanguard announced by staccato barking and sound of tiny clipped feet on the tile floor indicated the imminent arrival of my employer. Sure enough, there was her heavy rumbling tread.

The snuffling cotillion appeared, followed by their mistress in another brightly colored muumuu. Behind her, much more formally dressed, trailed a tall gentleman on the slender side with aquiline features and a faint trace of scent about him. High cheekbones and thick silvery hair which, I suspected, might once have been very dark, hinted at French or German blood in the family. She introduced us briefly, and I bowed slightly in my best steward mode.

Lloyd Bristol's smile was warm, revealing teeth too white and even to be real. His voice was soft, with a slight burr that bespoke of Northern England. "Glad to have you join us," he said. Availing himself of an armchair near the window, he took a set of reading glasses from his blazer pocket, opened the book he had been carrying, and began to read.

Lady Welsh settled herself in one of the sofas, where the four Pekinese promptly joined her, knocking each other over in an effort to lick her now-accessible face. Tabitha, the Pointer, lay down more properly on top of her feet. Ignoring Mr. Bristol, she carried on a running conversation with the dogs.

"Now, now, Yo Yo, that's your third biscuit. Mustn't be greedy, love... Melisande, now you must make room for Mitzi here too. Yes, yes, we can both get kisses, can't we? ... Pippa,... naughty, naughty, mustn't take Mummy's biscuits... Tabitha, you're such a good girl, you can have another little bite of Mummy's scone. Oh, yes, sweetie, we know you like lots of butter on it."

As I attempted to manoeuver gracefully around the exuberant dogs with my silver tray, she suddenly addressed me. "I trust your quarters are satisfactory?"

"Oh yes, madame; quite satisfactory, thank you." Satisfactory? The quarters were bloody palatial by my standards, even if I hadn't spent the last four years of my life living on board private yachts. Last night I had been shown to a separate cottage not far from the kitchen. A cottage, all my own! Yes, it was small, but even so, there was a bedroom, a sitting room, and a tiny kitchen. The bathroom alone was larger than most of the cabins I'd had to share with another crew member.

In fact, what awed me most about the Villa Bianco were

its enormous bathrooms: one of them, the master bath, was almost thirty feet across and twenty feet deep. Each was decorated almost entirely in tile, for there were no shower stalls—one just took a shower in the middle of the room. There was a shower head above, and a drain below, and the floor was pitched to the drain. To one side, there was a large tub, and the wall nearby had a series of glass shelves on which thick rolled towels were stacked. On another side, discreetly tucked behind a half-wall, sat a commode and bidet. A double sink completed the facilities. Bloody hell, I'd been in pubs smaller than these bathrooms.

But as I became familiar with the house, I noticed an odd thing—there didn't seem to be many personal items about. Perhaps I was used to the relative "clutter" of the boats, but there were none of the knick-knacks that one associates with much-loved homes—no squashy, comfy-looking cushions in a favorite chair, no books or collections of any sort; indeed no real bric-a-brac at all. Throughout the entire villa, I had seen only a handful of family photographs in silver frames. I asked Rudy about it over tea one day.

"Ah, the Villa Bianco, it is not hers," he said. "Lady Welsh, she has rented it for the season. She has had this house before, two years ago. No, she owns a house in Switzerland, which is where you will go in the summer."

I had been told that I would be expected to accompany them to Switzerland, but I hadn't heard when, and the news caught me by surprise. Summer season on the Côte d'Azur was *de rigueur* for the very wealthy. "Why would she go to Switzerland then?"

"Oh, she is not into the social scene. They do not, how would you say, go in much for the charity balls and such. She prefers to entertain small groups of people here. As you will see."

"What's the Swiss house like?"

"I have heard it is nice, though smaller than this. Me, I do not know, myself. I do not travel with her to Switzerland. She has another chef there. Quite a famous one."

"You have summers off, then?" I asked, doing the computations in my mind. In the South of France you could hire yourself out for the season and make a boatload of money.

"So to speak. I do a few private parties here and there, but mostly I go to England and see my family." A mist crept over his broad face at the mention of them. "My little children, they are growing so big. It is hard for me to be away from them so long." He pulled his wallet from his trousers, extracted a well-worn photograph, and handed it to me. A handsome blonde woman smiled broadly for the camera, her arms wrapped around two small girls aged perhaps five and seven. The older girl held a toddler on her lap. I had no difficulty in recognizing Rudy's wide-spaced dark eyes and thick black eyelashes in the faces of his children.

From a corner of the staff room came a sound that dispelled the moment.

"Awk!"

I jumped. "What was that?"

Rudy laughed. "That is Roger. You did not see him before?" He indicated a perch on which sat a large green parrot. "Watch out; Roger has the run—or do you say, the fly?—of the house."

I made a moue. "Who cleans up after him?"

He raised his expressive eyebrows and gave me a knowing look. "He, Mr. Bristol, does."

The parrot flapped to the back of Rudy's chair and climbed upon his shoulder, cocking an eye at the plateof biscuits near the tea pot. I hoped I wasn't allergic to parrots as well.

In addition to Rudy, Isobel, and myself, there were two other full-time staff who lived out, which is to say, off the premises—Madeleine, the chamber maid, and Cosimo, the gardener. There was almost no interaction between Lady Welsh and her other staff; certainly no idle conversation. Whilst her bath was being drawn, she went over her plans for the day with Isobel so the latter could have the proper clothes laid out at the proper time, but unless there was a substantial change in program wouldn't ring for her again. She spoke briefly to Rudy in the morning to go over the day's menu. Madeleine, and any other daily help we might have for special occasions, she never even saw. The whole lower level of the house was cleaned before they came down in the morning, which was generally about ten o'clock.

As butler and chauffeur, I was the only one who had much contact with Lady Welsh (who, incidentally, preferred to be addressed as Mrs. Bristol unless they were entertaining). If she wanted something and I was not in the room, she rang for me; silver and crystal bells were situated throughout the house for this purpose.

As the weeks passed, I became used to the daily routine at the Villa Bianco, which, on the whole, varied little. In the mornings I would attend to the cars. When I'd owned cars in England, I had always taken care of them myself, but these were Lady Welsh's fine automobiles. So within a week of my employment I had made the acquaintance of several other chauffeurs in the area and developed a telephone relationship with the customer service department of Rolls Royce to guard against my inadvertently damaging them. One of the first things I learned about car care on the Côte d'Azur was that I needed to wash, or at least wipe down the cars every day, because the red dust blown in from the Sahara, together with the salty air off the Mediterranean, played havoc with the paint job.

At half-past ten I would serve their morning coffee in the ornate silver coffee service (tea, at four o'clock, was served in a porcelain tea service) and find out their schedule for the day. It generally was our longest conversation of the day, and it might go something like this:

"Good morning, madame. Did you sleep well?"

"Good morning, Christopher. No, I'm afraid the wind kept me up. The branches were rubbing against the side of the house. Very unpleasant."

"I'll have it seen to, madame. What are your plans for today?"

"I have some correspondence to take care of. After that, so-and-so, the author, has a new book out, so I think I'll

## A Chaffeur's Twenty-Five Tips to a Perfect Car Finish

1. First, the obvious—whenever possible, try to garage the car.
2. Before getting started, remove rings, identity bracelets, and, most of all, your belt. More cars are scratched because of a belt buckle during washing than anywhere else.
3. Don't wear jeans, which tend to have rivets or metal buttons.
4. Make sure that the sponge used to wash your car is used only for that purpose. Sponges used for other types of cleaning will pick up dust or sand, which will damage the paint finish.
5. Make sure the end of the hose is plastic, not metal. If not, wrap it in duct tape.
6. Have ready two buckets, two sponges, and two chamois cloths.
7. Never wash a car in the hot sun; cold water from a hose pipe can crack a hot windshield. If the car has been standing in the sun, put it in the shade for a while first.
8. Take the keys out of the ignition and put them somewhere outside of the car. It's too easy to leave keys in the ignition with the radio going, then get called away and later find the battery dead. I've also had it happen that, while polishing the inside of the door, I've inadvertently hit the automatic door lock, then shut the door, locking the keys inside.
9. Make sure that all the windows and doors are fully closed.
10. Use only proprietary-brand car wash liquids, and stick with the same brand.
11. Prior to soaping, use lots of water at a reasonably high pressure spray to rinse the car. A thorough rinsing will remove the majority of grit, large dirt particles, or sand, all of which, if rubbed, can dull the paint finish.
12. When pre-rinsing, pay particular attention to the lower third of the body, the wheel arches, and beneath the door sills, where most road tar and dirt accumulate.

*(continued on next page)*

*(continued from previous page)*

13. Never let the car dry out or you will have water spots. If you notice it drying while you're soaping, start rinsing immediately.
14. Do your soaping in quarters, starting at the top. Leave the wheels till last, and use the second bucket of water and sponge for them. (Wheels collect more grit and brake-lining dust.)
15. When cleaning, don't forget the insides of door jambs, the interior of the trunk, the inside of the hood, and, if you have a hatchback, the channels.
16. For a finish free of water-spots, hold the hose (without a spray attachment) one inch from the surface. This creates a sheeting action which prevents the accumulation of large water droplets. Rinse thoroughly.
17. Use one chamois cloth expressly for windows. When it becomes grubby, use it for wiping the body of the car, and buy a new one for the windows. If the car is clean when the chamois is used, it shouldn't get black marks.
18. Use a separate rag and window cleaner (I prefer Windex Green, with vinegar) to clean wiper blades and black rubber surfaces.
19. Finish with Armor All on rubber, vinyl, and plastic surfaces. Use a hide food on leather surfaces, following the instructions on the tin.
20. Use a steel-wool pad infused with soap, such as SOS or Brillo, to clean whitewall tires.
21. Never put your sponge into water used with your SOS pad; you'll get iron filings in the sponge, which will rust and scratch.
22. If using an electric buffer, make sure you use exceptionally clean buffing bonnets. Change the bonnet regularly when buffing.
23. In cold climates, rinse the car after being out on salted roads, paying particular attention to the underside.
24. Cars that are used infrequently should be started once a week and left running for ten to fifteen minutes to keep debris from accumulating in the engine fluids, as well as to keep the battery fresh.
25. Reverse the direction of the car (back it in one week, pull it in forward the next) each week. This will prevent the tires from getting "flat spots" during long periods of inactivity.

relax and read until lunchtime in my study." The study was the Inner Sanctum. It was an unwritten rule that whilst in her study, Lady Welsh was not to be disturbed unless she rang.

"Mr. Bristol, however, will need to go into Monte Carlo; I have run out of my favorite chocolates. Then, after lunch, we shall be playing bridge with the Golightlys."

The Golightlys, inveterate bridge players like my employer, were Americans involved in the television industry who had rented in Monte Carlo for many years. "What time shall we expect them, madame?"

"They will arrive around two."

"Will they be staying for dinner?"

"No, I believe they have a cocktail party to attend elsewhere. We shall want dinner as usual at seven."

"Very good, madame."

If they had no plans elsewhere, I would set the table in the dining room with the luncheon china. I would serve them a gin and tonic at noon, followed at one o'clock by lunch, a fairly simple meal of salad or sandwiches unless they were entertaining. At four o'clock they had afternoon tea with scones, biscuits, and cakes, then an aperitif of sherry at six. Finally, there was a three- or four-course dinner at seven. It was no wonder Lady Welsh was the size she was.

As Rudy had said, they entertained regularly—often three or more nights a week. Her guests included makers of or heirs to fortunes made in liquor, broadcasting, and business, as well as writers and other *artistes,* patrons of the arts, and assorted titled aristocracy.

The formal dining room opened off the far end of the main hallway through a set of double entry doors. Although the room itself contained little else other than a long sideboard and a mahogany table that sat twenty people, its vista more than made up for its simplicity. One entire wall was comprised of French doors, which opened onto a veranda overlooking the spectacular gardens. Beyond, the coastline stretched back and away around Fourmis Bay, where the village of Beaulieu-sur-Mer was visible in the distance.

On one occasion I was amused to find that my former employer, Sir Graham Black, and his young wife were to be among the guests at a dinner party for sixteen. He didn't recognize me as I took her wrap at the door, and I made no attempt to introduce myself; I had ascertained that a professional butler, while quietly cordial, should be essentially invisible.

They presented quite a contrast. He was a slight, dried-apple of a man with glittery grey eyes, whose black evening attire only seemed to amplify his desiccated appearance. By contrast, his tall, chestnut-haired wife was easily the most attractive woman in the party. Outgoing and personable, she obviously enjoyed people, parties, and the wardrobe such a lifestyle required. When she excused herself to go to the powder room before dinner, all eyes followed her.

And sure enough, Sir Graham checked his watch.

Initially I had found it odd that I was not expected to valet Mr. Bristol, but there was never any question of my "doing" for him. I had no idea of his background, but I guessed by his speech that he must be highly educated; certainly he was incredibly well read. But he didn't seem to be financially independent. I assumed what few expenses he had, he could cover, but primarily it was she who ran the household; he was barely considered a factor in it. As a result, perhaps, I found him far more sympathetic than Lady Welsh. While she rarely acknowledged my presence, he would always greet me with a smile and a word or two. If I were driving him somewhere by himself, he would refuse my efforts to seat him in the back, preferring to sit in the passenger seat. He seemed to acknowledge, where Lady Welsh didn't, that things were changing in the servant sector and that lifestyles were less formal than they had once been. Sitting up front was his concession to the new order of staff.

The dogs, I learned quickly, were extremely friendly, especially at close range. The car was a good example. Unless I was running an errand on my own, there was always at least one of them with us. And like young children, they had to be

## Setting and Serving the Formal Dinner Party

- Individual menus at each place setting can be personalized, thereby doubling as place cards.
- Bread plates are placed to the left of the dinner plate, outside of the silverware, at approximately the place where one might rest an elbow (thus circumventing that from happening). Using the example of a clock face when indicating placement, the butter knife is placed across the plate, parallel to the table edge, with the blade toward the table edge and the handle on the right, at approximately three o'clock.
- Water goblets are placed above the main course knife. Wine glasses are placed to the right of the water goblets at about one o'clock; and if there is more than one of them, they trail toward the center of the table or form a loose triangle at the upper right-hand side of the dinner plate.
- A formal place setting utilizes a "service plate," a base plate of dinner size or perhaps a little larger on which the initial courses are set. The service plate remains on the table until the entrée is served, when it is removed together with the last course and replaced by the plate for the entrée. Because plates are exchanged for each course—which requires two hands—each guest is served one at a time. For example, the empty plate that held the fish course is lifted (together with the service plate) with the right hand from the guest's right side, and the left hand puts before her the plate bearing the entrée.
- In household silver service, where a butler presents a tray of food to the guest and then serves him from it, the platter is presented on the left. If more than one platter is required, the butler serves the entrée, followed by the maid or under-butler with the vegetables. Food is always served from the left, and plates are removed from the right. Wine and water are served from the right. Should it be necessary to add silverware, a knife is added from the right; forks, from the left.

*(continued on next page)*

*(continued from previous page)*

- The correct order of service is this. The lady of honor, who is seated on the host's right, is served first, and service moves counterclockwise around the table, serving the host last.
- Where there is no host, the hostess might designate an acting host, who is seated to the left of the lady of honor. In this case, service commences with the lady of honor and moves counterclockwise around the table to the acting host, skipping the hostess. The hostess is served last.
- At a large formal meal where there are many servers, the butler stands behind and slightly to right of the hostess' chair, except when pouring wine or giving direction to the servers under him.
- Regardless of whether plated or silver service is used, no serving dishes are ever put on the table, except an ornamental compote of fruit, nuts, or candy. Meat is carved in the kitchen; vegetables, bread, and condiments are passed and returned to the kitchen, the butler's pantry, or to a sideboard until there is no further call for them.
- There is a plate set before the guest at all times, until the end of the salad course. (In European fashion, the salad course follows the main course.) Following the salad course, all eating utensils and plates—including the bread plate—are removed, and the table is discreetly "crumbed," using a instrument resembling a thin spatula specially designed for that purpose, or a folded napkin and a small plate. Appropriate dessert silverware is then laid, and dessert plates are placed directly on the tablecloth.
- Coffee is properly served in the drawing room or living room, rather than the dining room.

in the front seat, where they could get to me. As I drove, there would be one under my elbow, one in my lap, one under my feet, one sniffing my left ear, and so on. Even Lady

Welsh, who preferred her dogs to anyone else, made no attempt to keep them away from me, even though their presence in the circumstances might impair my driving. Mr. Bristol, who was responsible for exercising them, apparently wasn't fond of exercise himself, for it was a regular occurrence for us to load the delighted dogs into the car and drive five minutes up the road to the park so that they could all go for "walkies." Each half-hour of exercise would result in nearly an hour of carefully hoovering the dog hair from the car, but I was the lucky one. Isobel, Terror of the Spanish Plains, had to wash each dog's paws and brush them for ages to remove the cat-o-nine-tails that would end up in their fur.

When one is regularly ambushed by five affectionate dogs to which one is allergic, there is a problem. But her complete formality with me precluded any thought of my saying nonchalantly, "I say, Lady W, I'm allergic to dogs; could you call them into the back seat, please?" Besides, I needed the job, and so I suffered. However, because of my continual snuffling, so did Lady Welsh.

One afternoon we were out in the car, bound for her regular hair appointment. I was so used to my allergic reactions that I wasn't even aware that I had been itching and sneezing until Lady Welsh spoke impatiently from the back seat.

"Why are you always sniffling?"

Caught off guard, I searched for a way to impart the news without getting myself sacked. "It seems to happen, madame, in confined spaces when the dogs are very close."

"Oh, we can't have that," she said, offended. "There's nothing dirty about my dogs." This was true; Isobel brushed them every morning and gave them baths twice a week. "You can go to my allergist."

"I'm not sure it will help, madame," I began. "I've been to many allergists—"

"My allergist will cure you," she said with finality.

Her allergist had offices in Cannes on the Côte d'Azur equivalent of Harley Street. Comprised entirely of tile and plastic, the office was stark and impersonal. I was directed to a three-foot square cubicle with a plastic shower curtain and told to undress completely.

After five minutes—which feels like fifteen, when you're naked as the day you were born and freezing your extremities off—a doctor in a white laboratory coat pulled back the curtain, looked in, and said straightaway, "Ah, neuroatopic eczema. We can cure that. Put your clothes back on."

My jaw dropped at his brilliance. That was the quickest diagnosis I had ever had. I dressed quickly.

In the corridor he gave me a rapid outline of the lifestyle I should be leading, one that included no curtains or rugs in my room, plastic mattress covers on my bed topped by pure cotton sheets, and only cotton or silk clothes. "No teddy bears from your girlfriend," he warned. "Dust is your enemy."

I must have looked horrified at the impossibility of putting such a prescription into practice, because he patted my shoulder and handed me prescriptions for two types of pills and a cream to alleviate the sneezing and itching. He then added, "And stay as far away as possible from animals."

His five-minute consultation cost me a week's wages, but the result allowed me to continue working for Lady Welsh.

Quite often Lady Welsh's day's schedule would include a trip into Monte Carlo, Cannes, or Ventimiglia for some shopping and lunch. Her purchases were rarely large; a trinket, some chocolates, an unusual piece of jewelry that caught her eye. She almost never bought clothing, but then, she was far from a fashion plate. She wore muumuus or caftans or the odd pantsuit that suited her figure. Mr. Bristol almost always accompanied her on her excursions. Sometimes he did a little shopping of his own, returning with a small carrier bag containing, perhaps, a tie, a pair of gloves, or socks.

Each Thursday I drove them to the Hôtel de Paris in Monte Carlo so that she could have her hair done for the weekend. This was evidently force of habit, since the activities of their weekends were indistinguishable from those the rest of the week.

The century-old Hôtel de Paris was a study in old elegance, its spun-sugar Rococo facade giving evidence of the grandeur inside. In the foyer there was a bronze statue of Louis XV on horseback. Because it was traditional to touch the horse for luck before an evening of gaming in the casino next door, the nose and fetlock gleamed brightly on the otherwise dark statue. Inside, the spacious, high-ceilinged lobby dripped opulence, the atmosphere almost purposefully intimidating to anyone other than the extremely wealthy. As I pulled up, the liveried doormen would spring to open the doors of the Rolls and greet Mr. and Mrs. Bristol warmly.

Although in practice just a glorified valet parking attendant, being a doorman of a fine hotel on the Côte d'Azur was a highly coveted job. The tipping potential was so great that jobs were either passed down, father to son, or sold to the highest bidder. The doormen maintained an inexplicable caste system all their own. It was remarkable how, even on a crowded Saturday night, a doorman could always find a parking spot for someone famous. Or better yet, someone rich and famous. Even though I'm sure it was the size of the tip that made all the difference, just being rich wouldn't do it.

After a while, I could get parking spots at the restaurants and hotels such as the Hôtel de Paris. While not, perhaps, a spot in front, the doormen weren't foolish: Mr. and Mrs. Bristol were regulars every year in Monte Carlo. And whereas a prince may come in once a year to attend the Red Cross Gala, the society event of the year, Lady Welsh was there every week and knew the people on the door. Mr. Bristol would give the doorman a tip for opening the car door upon their arrival, then another for holding the hotel door on the way out. But in the meantime, I'd have slipped him an additional ten francs.

"Did you give him anything?" Mr. Bristol would enquire sternly, later.

"No, sir," I'd lie. I knew that nothing, but nothing, got done in the South of France without copious tipping. My ten francs went towards the doorman's goodwill and insured I got a parking spot.

A lot of my time was spent waiting outside whenever they

were in public, be it a shopping excursion, the theater, or one of the occasional benefit galas. I'd read a book in the passenger seat, or talk to the doormen or other chauffeurs, always keeping a close watch on my car. Except in front of the Hôtel de Paris, one would never leave an expensive car unattended because someone might key it, since the "other half"— the common populace—were almost communistic in their hate of the rich and of anything ostentatious. In fact, because the Rolls had had stones thrown at it during my predecessor's employ, Lady Welsh preferred I not wear a chauffeur's cap. Those who made their living in private service were seen by the leftist movement to be selling out by being a lackey to someone else; a chauffeur, identifiable by his traditional flat dark cap, was too much of a statement.

I had similar problems with the Buick station wagon, which to the average Frenchman was a vulgar display of power. Especially when Mr. and Mrs. Bristol would dine out with the Golightlys, Lady Welsh would insist that we collect them in the Buick. The American car was so wide and the village roads so narrow that I could appreciate the native point of view; driving on the pavement literally added insult to injury.

My day off began after tea had been cleared away Sunday afternoon, and continued until Monday night. I'd visit the yachties with whom I'd become friends when working as a steward. Mostly we would all end up playing darts at the pub while Darlene dispensed drinks and a good dose of home. I missed the camaraderie of my mates from the boats. While I had met some other household staff in my new job, there hadn't been anyone interesting, anyone I could call a friend, and certainly no one my age. Yet unwise judgment on my part regarding my yachtie mates nearly lost me my position.

On New Year's Eve, I was to drive Lady Welsh, Mr. Bristol, and six of their friends to a party at the Hôtel de Paris. With a party of that size, we took the Buick, which had a second, backward-facing rear seat, which folded down into the bed when not in use. Even so, this meant that Mr.

Bristol and one of the other men needed to ride up in the front with me, a highly unusual situation, but one necessary as no one wanted to drive on New Year's Eve. Wending my way through the crowded streets around the Square Beaumarchais, I dropped them off at 9:00 P.M. "Pick us up here at half past twelve," Mr. Bristol instructed, as he followed the party into the hotel.

Parking would be impossible, even with my ten-franc-induced build-up of goodwill. With a three-and-a-half hour reprieve and no hope of finding a spot for the large car, I had an idea.

I pulled up in front of the Bar des Anglais, feeling very smart in my chauffeur's black suit and tie. "I'm off for a few hours, and I've got the station wagon," I told the lads. "Care for a drink at the Villa Bianco?" Without hesitation, seven of my mates piled into the Buick, and I drove back to the estate and showed them round the property. After the tour I brought out the champagne, and we went through a number of bottles in my sitting room.

Since I was driving, I drank only two glasses of champagne. But I was high on the moment. For the first time since I'd left England, I had a place I could bring people back to; for security reasons, yacht owners never permitted crew to bring people onto the boats unless you had known them a long time. This was my first house, and I was so proud. I had a real job. I wasn't transient anymore, nor unemployed with no prospects.

Shortly before midnight I took the lads back to the Bar des Anglais, where we counted down the minutes to the New Year, then I left to collect Lady Welsh and her party at the Hôtel de Paris. After driving around for some minutes, I finally double-parked the Buick in front of the hotel and waited for my employers. It was a balmy, perfect night, with a slight breeze blowing up from the sea, and I had the windows down, enjoying it.

At twenty minutes to one, Mr. Bristol came out. The four men were half carrying Lady Welsh, so I guessed she had had a good time. I got out of the car to help them with her, while the doorman sprang to open the tailgate. Mr. Bristol flipped the catch, releasing the backward-facing seat, which had been unexpectedly folded back down. Suddenly he uttered an exclamation of surprise and disgust.

"Oh my God. What's *this*?"

I looked in horror. The unmistakable stench of vomit rose from the floor where one of my mates had been sick and hadn't told me.

Speechless with dread, I spent the first few hours of January first cleaning the back of the car while Mr. Bristol stood by, reprimanding me. I was sure I would be starting the new year off unemployed.

"You must *think*—if your friends would do this to the car, who knows what they might have done to the house?" he chastized.

Then he softened and said kindly, "We like you, but you're very young yet. You have to realize that when *we* play, *you* work."

It was a lesson I've never forgotten.

# 6

# Lifestyles of the Rich and Not-So-Famous

Every Friday at quarter to twelve, I drove Lady Welsh and Mr. Bristol to the Villa El Patio in Cannes for their weekly lunch with Mrs. Florence J. Gould. Mrs. Gould, the widow of Frank Jay Gould, whose father, Jay, had been a railway magnate in the States, was a well-known patron of the arts. Her wealth made my employer look middle-class by comparison.

As the Rolls pulled into the semicircular driveway in front of the angular, slightly Moroccan-looking stucco house, we would set off a bell in the servant's hall. This warning allowed Mrs. Gould's butler, Copley, to be waiting outside the front entrance to greet Mrs. Gould's guests and show them into the house. I would deposit Lady Welsh and Mr. Bristol into Copley's care, then continue round the back and park. Then, by entering through the servant's entrance, I'd come into the large kitchen where a chef, his assistant, and a kitchen maid would be putting the final touches to lunch preparations.

As size went, the kitchen could have supplied a large hotel, and was similarly appointed. In addition to an island with an auxiliary vegetable sink, there were two vast stainless-steel prep tables lining one long wall, two six-burner Wolf commercial stoves, and two double wall ovens. The staff room beyond, thick with many layers of white paint, was furnished with a television, well-worn overstuffed chintz furniture, and a dining table that would easily seat eight.

On most Fridays, Lady Welsh and Mr. Bristol were Mrs. Gould's only guests, but occasionally she would invite one or two others to join them. This meant I would have company for lunch, since, quite properly, the house staff would already have eaten. I very much looked forward to Friday lunches, because whatever was being served to Mrs. Gould and her guests in the dining room, both the house and visiting staff would have as well—even if it were fresh fois gras, turbot bon femme, a seafood platter, or fillets of beef.

Copley showed me round the ground floor one day when Mrs. Gould and Lady W were dining in the garden. Although not by Côte d'Azur standards an enormous villa—I would guess that it had only five bedrooms—El Patio was nevertheless spacious, and its contents made it spectacular.

In the lobby off the front entrance, gleaming marble floors highlighted a double curved staircase that led to an open landing above. The long rectangular Grand Salon and dining room that opened off the foyer looked like large corridors, and muted light from the tall, multipaned windows illuminated old tapestries and oil paintings that even I could recognize as important Impressionist artwork. Lush white rugs adorned the honey-colored parquet floors. The dining room looked as though it could seat forty people.

Although in her eighties, Mrs. Gould was still an avid collector of antiques, artwork, and jewelry; and her enormous wealth had allowed her to satisfy her wide and varied interests. The feeling one had of the house was one of being surrounded with beautiful things. In every room of the house her vast collections of paintings, drawings, books, and medieval objects were showcased. An ornate French mantle clock above one fireplace featured a gilded clock face atop the back of a rhinoceros. Polished Louis XV table surfaces were covered with collectibles and *objets d'art*—Oriental vases and porcelain figurines, a collection of jade in colors of pink, green, and white. Later I heard that only a week before her death, Mrs. Gould had bought a quarter of a million dollars' worth of Chinese jade.

In the basement she had built a private place of worship. The pews, Copley told me, had been purchased from the papal palace in Avignon, and there was an altar where each Sunday a priest would come to El Patio to offer a solitary service for her.

Mrs. Gould's butler's pantry was something to behold, and Copley was justifiably proud of it. Showcased in built-in cabinets faced with leaded glass were, literally, dozens of different sets of porcelain dinner plates, a large collection of cups and saucers, and many complete table services, some with intricately laced, interwoven basket-weave edges. I could recognize the names of Sèvres and Limoges, but most of the patterns were Oriental and completely new to me. Copley pointed out a stack of soft white plates decorated with a flowery pattern. "That is Chien Lung," he said, to my puzzled look. "And these," he indicated a complete service for perhaps twenty-four, "Napoleon had made as a gift to Josephine."

On other shelves were full sets of antique Venetian glassware, some dating back hundreds of years. As I was admiring the intricate patterns, Copley brought forth a polished wooden case from the cupboard beneath the display cabinets.

"Have you ever seen one of these?"

Nestled in velvet lining was what appeared to be a block of glass, somewhat like those used in building shower walls. Mystified, I shook my head.

"Each one of these sets of glassware comes with a spare, uncut block of crystal. In case—God forbid!—there's a breakage, we can have the replacement cut so that the same crystal is used for all."

God forbid, indeed. Needless to say, with all that wealth tied up in china and crystal, every precaution was taken to ensure their safety. All of the sinks in the scullery were lined with specially cut plastic sheets, so that if, by chance, one of the servants knocked a glass or plate against the side of the sink, the liner would absorb the shock. Further, all of Mrs. Gould's staff were on a bonus program. At year end she would inventory Copley's pantry, and if there were no chips or breakages, everyone would receive an additional month's wages in addition to their already generous Christmas bonuses.

I gaped at this. In Lady Welsh's household, there were no Christmas bonuses. Christmas Day was a full working day, complete with the making and serving of Christmas dinner for however many friends and family were in attendance. On Christmas Eve, after their dinner had been cleared away, all the staff were summoned to the drawing room, where Lady Welsh's artificial Christmas tree was set up. We were offered a drink (which we refused; it wasn't seemly to drink in the presence of your employer) while she distributed to us a package apiece. The previous Christmas my package had contained a garish, brightly colored Kenzo sweater in which I would never, ever have been seen, even had it been the proper size.

Mrs. Gould died in 1983 while I was working for Lady Welsh, and for months the disposition of her estate, estimated at nearly $124 million, was the talk of the South of France. While she had left a will, there were no heirs; Mrs. Gould had no children, and had outlived most of her friends. Hence, the will stipulated that with the exception of a few individual bequests, all of her antiques, jewelry, and art collections were to be auctioned. The proceeds were to go to a foundation in her name which would be used primarily to promote Franco-American friendship and understanding.

The mindful attention shown by her servants to her beloved possessions didn't go unrewarded. Her generosity to her staff was quickly known "round the back stair": Copley and the rest of Mrs. Gould's servants each ended up with a substantial endowment in trust, distributed for the rest of their lives.

Another bequest was that a portrait of Mrs. Gould go to Lady Welsh. In the portrait she was wearing huge sapphires

## From the Butler's Pantry: Tips on Care of Fine China, Crystal, and Silver

- Fine stemware should not be washed in a dishwasher. Wash crystal stemware by hand, using warm soapy water and mild soap. Research has shown repeated washing in very hot water with detergents can damage the surface polish of crystal.
- Wash one piece at a time. Do not soak a number of glasses in a sink at one time; they're likely to be cracked or chipped.
- Polish a glass by holding it loosely by the base, your hand covered by a lint-free cloth. With the other hand, take the other end of the cloth and rub the interior and exterior of the bowl gently. *Do not, however, use a twisting motion* which can create undue pressure on the stem. In this way, not only do your hands not touch the glass, they are protected from any possible chips in the rim of the glass.
- Change the cloth often; a wet cloth will leave streaks.
- Never place glasses upside down on a draining board, or when storing. The finely made rims are the most fragile part of the crystal.
- Certain kinds of water leave lime deposits. Rub marks on crystal glasses or goblets with half a lemon, or use white vinegar, applied with a cloth.
- To remove red wine stains from a crystal decanter, pour one third to one half cup uncooked white rice into the decanter and cover it with soapy water or white vinegar. Shake vigorously—the rice acts as an abrasive—then let sit several hours. Rinse with clean warm water and dry.
- Dry decanters by filling a nylon stocking with silica gel crystals. Roll it very thin and stuff it into the decanter neck, pushing down until the stocking touches the bottom. Pull up when dry.
- Never put gold- or silver-rimmed china in the microwave.

*(continued on next page)*

*(continued from previous page)*

- Because in stacking or handling, plates can be scratched when slid over one another, store china with a pad of some sort between plates. The pad can be felt, bubble wrap, even a paper towel.
- Plates slid together under water can be even more easily scratched.
- Fine china should be washed by hand using a mild detergent, then rinsed immediately with clean hot water. Do not let plates soak for long periods of time in water containing a detergent of any kind.
- Keep an inventory on a small notecard of china and crystal glasses on each shelf of the china closet. If something breaks, correct the card. Replace broken china as soon as it breaks if possible, in case the pattern is discontinued.
- Because eggs characteristically will turn silver eating utensils black, clean utensils immediately after use.
- Do not leave salt in silver salt dishes or unlined salters overnight, as the salt will eventually corrode the silver. Salters lined with blue glass will not be marred.
- Store silver in felt bags to discourage tarnishing. Silver cupboards and drawers lined with brown felt help keep the silver clean. Smaller items can be stored in airtight plastic bags. Use a straw to suck out the excess air.
- Flatware that is dishwasher-safe should be placed in dishwasher baskets separate from gadgets and utensils. The latter might have nonstainless parts that could rust and mar the flatware if they are in the same basket.

on her ears, throat, wrist, and fingers. The central sapphire in the necklace, I learned later, was called "The Blue Princess" and weighed over 114 carats. It was suspended from three other diamond-encircled sapphires weighing twenty-four to forty carats each. While Mrs. Gould had seldom been seen without some of her extensive cache of precious jewelry on, I thought the sapphires quite the most spectacular I had ever seen.

Both Sotheby's and Christie's, the London-based auction concerns, sought the opportunity to auction Mrs. Gould's estate. Sotheby's eventually sold her antiques, books, and artwork, while Christie's won the chance to auction her jewelry. It was there, I was told, that the famed necklace figured in yet another interesting postscript. During an exhibition of the jewels in London, two gentlemen in very expensive suits walked into the auctioneer's sale-rooms. They had with them a case containing a matched set of Purdey shotguns, which they professed to be interested in selling. But things moved quickly once the gun-case was opened. Brandishing the Purdeys, which were in fact loaded, the men forced staff and visitors to the floor and demanded the jewels. That the jewels were, in fact, accessible—they were to be moved to another safe very shortly—was later thought to be indicative the thieves may have had inside information.

An astute young jewelry expert prevented what would have been a huge robbery. At gunpoint, she was bringing forth the tray of jewels, when she suddenly slumped into a faint, scattering the contents of the tray on the carpet in front of her. The thieves, conscious of the time, hastily grabbed up the gems. But the quick-witted woman had "fainted" on top of the Blue Princess, saving the necklace from robbery. The gunmen actually made away with few items, none of them major Gould pieces. At its subsequent auction in New York City, April 1984, Mrs. Gould's jewelry netted her foundation over eight million dollars. The necklace containing the Blue Princess sold for $1,320,000.

Few people in the world have resources like Mrs. Gould, and jobs in households such as hers were coveted and rarely were vacant. Although I knew it unrealistic to aspire to similar benefits with Lady Welsh, it was partly through exposure to El Patio that I began to see how, er, penurious my employer was.

I had been in Lady Welsh's employ for a little over a year when, one morning, Isobel returned from serving their breakfast and handed me an envelope.

"What is this?" I was puzzled.

"From Her," she answered, with a sniff. Isobel always referred to Mrs. Bristol in Capital Letters.

I opened it and found a short, handwritten missive on her engraved letterhead: "You have performed your duties in a satisfactory manner, and have shown an aptitude for your work. Therefore, effective immediately, you shall be considered a full butler, and your salary shall be increased by £5 per week."

While pleased at the only compliment I had ever received from her, I snorted at the pay rise. Five pounds was the equivalent of one cassette tape or four pints of beer.

Lady Welsh preferred to shop in Italy, where prices were thirty to forty percent cheaper than in France—to say nothing of Switzerland, where everything was even more expensive. So each Friday we drove to Ventimiglia, just over the border on the Italian Riviera, for the weekly open-air market. The Ventimiglia marketplace consisted of a series of stalls selling everything from fresh produce and flowers to leather goods, clothing, jewelry, and souvenirs. It was a bustling cacophonous atmosphere—hoards of people jostled each other in front of produce and meat stalls, their voices raised as they haggled over items, while the highly diverse smells of blossoms, leather goods, aged cheeses, and humanity assailed the nose. Much of the merchandise on sale in the streets of Ventimiglia were knockoffs; on a walk from one end of the marketplace to the other one would encounter ten professional con artists hawking fake name-brand luggage, scarves, and Rolex watches to unsuspecting tourists.

The primary objective of our Italian excursions was to buy liquor. We were allowed to bring back into France a gallon of spirits per person, so each week we returned with an assortment of scotch, vodka, or gin. Lady Welsh was, I understood, stocking up for the summer in Switzerland, where scotch that might cost the equivalent of $60 there could be purchased in Italy for only $15. Occasionally the Golightlys would go with them, allowing Lady Welsh to bring back two additional gallons of booze.

For all the restrictions on the amount of liquor that could be brought back into France, the French authorities never actually checked our purchases at the border. But I learned the hard way that it was a far different story in Switzerland.

In April we began to make arrangements to transport the household to Lady Welsh's Swiss residence. As her Côte d'Azur residences were rented, relatively little outside of clothing and personal effects had to be packed for travel, and for this Isobel was responsible. She, Lady Welsh, the five dogs, and Roger the parrot would take the Rolls Royce, while Mr. Bristol drove the Mercedes and a nephew of hers drove the Mini. I was to drive the Buick station wagon, which would contain all the booze accumulated from our excursions to Italy over the winter.

Rudy and one of the daily housemen packed the car, loading the liquor anywhere they could find room: under seats, down wheel wells, under the spare tire. They covered it all with suitcases full of clothing. The large car sagged over its wheels.

Since we would be in Switzerland until late October, and because I had two days off due me once I got there, my girlfriend Deirdre was driving up with me for the weekend. She and I would, I thought, have a lovely, leisurely six-hour drive all to ourselves. Then together we could explore the Swiss countryside, perhaps even do some skiing near Lake Geneva. I hadn't asked permission for this, but I thought, what harm could it do?

It was a bright spring day when we started off. As we progressed northward, the air became brisk, and patches of unmelted snow were visible in shady areas. Just outside Montélimar, we stopped for a picnic along the side of the road. I was excited and proud that, through my job, we could take this little holiday together. And I was just a little smug that I had managed to turn what would surely have been a long, boring, solitary ride into a nice trip.

Some four to five hours later we neared the border station that heralded the entrance to Switzerland. As I watched, the three vehicles ahead of us were waved through with only cursory glances. Then I pulled forward to where the guard stood and handed him my British and Deirdre's Irish passports.

For a long moment his flat grey eyes assessed the Buick. Then he pointed to a corrugated iron Quonset hut, where several official vehicles stood. "Please drive over there," he said. My stomach began to churn.

"Would you please step out of the car." It wasn't a request. Deirdre and I obliged quickly.

"Please remove the luggage from the car." My hands were clammy as I lifted one piece after another of matched Louis Vuitton luggage, setting it in neat rows to one side. Still, the car sat low on its wheels, looking to my eyes like a bloated pig. "If you would now drive over there, onto the scale," he indicated the iron rectangle sunk into the asphalt.

The Buick was six hundred pounds overweight.

"You will wait inside one moment, please," he said, and spoke into a walkie-talkie. We were ushered into the Quonset hut, where an official took our passports from the guard and began making notations on a tablet in front of him. Within a few minutes, a second guard appeared, towing a flat trailer, and the two of them began pulling the car apart. Load after load of booze was brought forth, until the trailer was nearly filled. I watched helplessly, humiliated beyond words and fearful of what was going to happen. I'd never been in trouble with the authorities in my life.

"Are you starting a restaurant?" There was no humor in the question. The Swiss are not a humorous people.

"No, sir," I whispered. "I-I'm a butler." My mouth was dry, though my shirt certainly wasn't. "I'm on my way to my employer's house."

"Are you saying the liquor doesn't belong to you?"

"Yes, sir. I mean, no, sir. It belongs to my employer."

The guard questioned me thoroughly, until I believed that in addition to a fine, I was going to jail. The fine alone was more than I made in five months. And I couldn't be sure Lady Welsh would pay it, or take responsibility.

If a butler's job is to shield his employer from unpleasantness, I had certainly failed this time. However, some forty-five minutes later, much to my relief, Deirdre and I were released. But instead of seventy-odd bottles of smuggled liquor to deliver to my employer, I had only a receipt indicating their confiscation by the Swiss border patrol, and a court summons in her name.

Several weeks later, because the judge who was to hear the case was the companion of a great friend of hers, Lady Welsh was allowed to settle the case out of court. Her fine was reduced to only 3,000 Swiss francs, about $1,500, for the incident. But she remained irrationally convinced that I had been caught because Deirdre had been with me, that her Irish passport had somehow sparked an investigation of our cargo. "And you had no right to take her. You were *working*," she accused.

And needless to say, each time she had to purchase the far more expensive Swiss scotch, I heard about it.

Built on a hillock from which one could see Lake Geneva at a distance, the Maison des Fleurs was a ranch-style dwelling of cream-colored stucco interspersed with brick, crowned with a heavy Spanish tile roof. A flower-lined drive of perhaps three hundred feet ascended from the automatic gates at the bottom of the hill to the square parking area in front of the unprepossessing house. But as its name suggested, the grounds were awash with vivid floral borders; in addition to the ubiquitous red geraniums the Swiss favored as a means of keeping flies away, there were masses of brightly colored annuals in planters throughout the property. Tree and shrub roses of every color abounded. I recognized waxy, ruby-colored begonias, lipstick-pink impatiens, fat pale pink and white peonies, and satiny pansies peeping through the low-growing shrubbery.

While it appeared to be a single-storied house, because it was built on a hill there were actually several levels inside. A pair of heavy wooden entry doors accented with leaded glass opened into the wide foyer. Corridors led right to bedrooms and left to the kitchen, pantry, and staff room. Continuing straight from the foyer, one stepped down into the long dining room; beyond it two stairs led into the spacious sitting room. Open-beam ceilings and a brick fireplace dramatized the space. Huge picture windows overlooked the large rectangular pool, which was set flush into a pebble-dash deck and surrounded by a lush green lawn edged with more flower borders. Isobel and I occupied quarters downstairs, which were partially underground, but with a view of a private garden. A full-time chef, a daily maid, and a gardener all lived off the premises.

Although considerably smaller than the villas Lady Welsh rented in the South of France, the furnishings of Maison des Fleurs were far more beautiful. The dining room was furnished with hand-carved mahogany chairs upholstered in ornate brocades. Gold-leaf frames set off dark oil paintings and antique mirrors, while the walls were accented with gilded wall sconces. A bow-fronted chest embellished with inlaid marquetry stood in the front hall opposite a magnificent marble-topped sideboard. Easily six feet long, the top of the sideboard was actually comprised of marble pieces forming a mosaic that depicted a bird in the center, surrounded by small scenes of people and landscapes.

Unlike the Villa Bianco, this was a warm, lived-in house, albeit slightly dated. The overstuffed sofas and chairs in the sitting room, while clean and fresh, were covered in fabric reminiscent of another era and accented with big fluffy pillows. A collection of turtles of every kind—glass, clay, porcelain, even stone—sat on tables and bookshelves.

Life was much calmer in Switzerland, due, in part, to the fact that Maison des Fleurs was definitely in the country. Surrounding the house were pastures on gently rolling hills, much of it planted with grapes for wine. As in France, I took care of the cars and drove my employers wherever they wished to go; but on the whole, I was less of a chauffeur and more of a butler while in Switzerland. On Fridays I drove them into nearby Lausanne, where Lady Welsh had her hair done. Mostly, however, they stayed in, reading books and the papers by the swimming pool, writing and receiving letters, and visiting with guests.

The manner of entertaining differed as well. Guests would come for a week or a fortnight rather than for an evening, and dinners in particular were very formal. I found the variety of visitors enjoyable; Mr. and Mrs. Bristol knew some interesting people, many old film stars, composers, and literati. It was no hardship for me to serve tea or meals to a few extra diners each day. But it did mean more work for Isobel, because Lady Welsh's rules were that breakfast was always taken in their rooms, never in the dining room.

Roger, the parrot, had a large cage in the sitting room, but only during dinner parties was the door closed on its occupant. The rest of the day it would not be unusual to find Roger regarding you from the top of the elaborate brocade draperies, the finial on the antique rosewood secretary, or the arm of one of the sofas. Further, if Isobel or I went into town, we were expected to take Roger with us, "to give him an outing." On these excursions Roger rode on the back of the driver's seat, occasionally culling a hair from my head and proclaiming "Awk!" into my ear at unexpected moments.

He seemed to have a keen sense of smell for anything that had sugar in it, for he invariably appeared in the staff room when we were having tea, or when the chef was preparing sweets. I would move my ironing board and clean linen as far away from him as possible, and reach for the biscuit tin. Roger's favorite treat was a McVitie's chocolate covered biscuit, and I loved watching him eat it. Holding the cookie in one stubby black claw, he would carefully cull away the chocolate, occasionally closing his bright eyes slowly, as if in ecstasy. When only the shortbread biscuit underneath remained, he would cock his head and peer at the offending cookie with an air of disfavor, then drop it imperiously on the floor.

Whilst in Switzerland, I noticed a relaxing of the tension between Isobel and myself. She began to acknowledge, then even speak to me when our paths crossed in the staff room. Whether this was due to the slower pace of life experienced at Maison des Fleurs or an acceptance of the fact I was going to be in this position awhile, I never knew. Or perhaps it had something to do with the chef, who was a great friend of hers.

Marco Rossini was, I learned through Isobel, the best private chef money could buy. Although he was only in his mid-forties, he cooked the annual dinner held for the Club de Cent, an exclusive club comprising one hundred of Europe's best chefs. Tall and slender with thinning hair, a sharp nose, and the long delicate fingers of a surgeon, Marco loved what he did and it showed in each creation. He had, he told me over coffee one morning, once worked for the Aga Khan.

"The Aga Khan!" I echoed, wide-eyed. "Why did you leave?"

"I have a wife and two children," he said. Although he spoke with an Italian accent, his English was perfect, and now a touch of pride crept into his surprisingly deep voice. "The Aga Khan is more than fair in his compensation, but he requires staff that will travel with him all the time. I soon tired of it. I missed my family."

"And so you came to work here," I prompted.

He nodded, pouring another cup of his strong black coffee. His hazel eyes grew mischievous. "But it didn't end there. A few years later the Aga Khan called and asked me to return. He told me he would triple whatever Lady Welsh was paying me."

"And you didn't take it?" The thought was inconceivable.

Marco said he had gone to Lady Welsh and explained the offer. "I cannot compete with him," she had answered. "But it will be a great thing for you. You must go."

So, he said, after negotiating a contract for a fixed amount of time, he had gone; and the money he'd made by the time he returned allowed him to dictate his own terms. Now he owned a huge apartment in nearby Monnaz, worked six months of the year for Lady Welsh, and part-time for someone in Geneva the rest of the year.

There was a muted rush of air as Roger, the parrot, flapped into the staff room and landed on the back of one of the kitchen chairs.

"Awk!" he cried.

It was as profound a response as anything I could have said.

# 7

# Life "Below Stairs"

Working with Marco was a wonderful experience, and it was a pleasure to serve his exquisite productions to Mr. and Mrs. Bristol and their guests. Not only was he extraordinarily creative, he concentrated on details such as the presentation of a dish. His concern over the latter made for some interesting displays.

We had a dinner party scheduled for eight people one night, and Marco and I were occupied in our respective ways in its preparation. As they often did, the meal had a theme. This particular evening's menu was planned around wild fowl in season, and the morning of the party, Marco was fretting about how to present the butter.

I was polishing the silver in the adjacent butler's pantry as he devised, and then discarded, various ideas.

"No, no, I've done that before," he said aloud, as he paced the length of the kitchen, moving, as always, with the grace of a dancer. "I need something truly *recherché.*" Then abruptly he stopped, brightening.

"I've got it! I've got it!" he shouted, and ran out of the house. I listened to his Saab roar down the driveway.

A quarter of an hour later he returned, carrying, to my

astonishment, a collection of his young son's rubber ducks. These he washed, cut in half, filled with the softened butter, and chilled.

That night, molded butter ducks of graduated size on "ponds" of blue china plates formed a neat line down the center of the table.

I remember the dinner party well, although its menu was no more complex than most of Marco's culinary triumphs. As a first course, I brought round what looked to be an elaborate white cake, but was in actuality a tall ice ring decorated with round ice balls, into which Marco had frozen a shallow silver bowl. This was filled with Beluga caviar, and on the silver tray round the base, lemon rings and radish roses alternated with the blini on which the guests spread the caviar. I carried the sour cream that topped the caviar blini in a silver creamer in my other hand.

The second course was fresh foie gras, layered in the center of a platter that was decorated with triangles of aspic all the way round and highlighted by a bird's nest at each end. The birds' nests were made of shoestring potatoes and contained tiny cooked quails' eggs. A small scoop of fresh lemon sorbet served in a tiny coupé dish followed as a palate cleanser before the main course.

Roast pheasant, decorated with the reserved tail feathers, had been carved and reassembled over wild rice. Although the presentation was beautiful, serving it was tricky—more than once I worried about tickling a guest in the ear with the pheasant's long, showy tail feathers. The fresh vegetables that accompanied the bird included buttered baby brussels sprouts a mere half-inch in diameter, julienne carrots, sugar snap peas, and piped duchess potatoes that had been browned under the broiler.

After a blessedly simple salad course, I brought forth Marco's *pièce de résistance,* individual Grand Marnier soufflés. Not surprisingly, everyone passed on the cheese course, finishing with cordials and coffee.

Marco's sweets and confections were legendary among Lady Welsh's guests, especially when he accented them with

### Individual Grand Marnier Soufflés

*Serves 8*

8 egg yolks at room temperature, lightly beaten
⅔ cup sugar, plus more to coat soufflé dishes
½ cup Grand Marnier liqueur
10 egg whites, at room temperature
¼ tsp. cream of tartar

Preheat oven to 400° F. Fill a 13" x 9" x 2" baking dish with 1 inch of boiling water and place into hot oven while you prepare soufflé.

Butter the bottom and sides of eight four-inch (8 oz.) soufflé dishes (ramekins), then add sugar to coat.

Using a bain-marie or double boiler, bring water to a boil in lower pan. In upper pan, add egg yolks and sugar and beat about five minutes over low heat until a ribbon of about one inch forms when you lift the spoon from the pan. Add Grand Marnier and mix well. Cool over ice water, beating to cool more quickly.

To the bowl of a stand mixer add egg whites and cream of tartar. Beat on "high" until stiff peaks form when whisk is lifted out. *Do not overbeat.* Fold carefully into the Grand Marnier mixture, using a large spatula and using a turn-and-fold motion to mix well. Pour into prepared ramekins, filling approximately two-thirds full.

Place dishes into the 13" x 9" x 2" baking dish with boiling water (which will have reduced somewhat). Bake six to eight minutes, or until soufflés have risen approximately one inch above the rim of the ramekins and are a light golden color. Serve immediately.

(Soufflés can be prepared in advance to the point of needing the egg whites whipped and folded in.)

spun sugar tops. These were quite a production, but then, Marco didn't take shortcuts.

"But it isn't difficult, " he assured me one day. "Come, I'll show you how it's done."

As I watched, he set about lining the kitchen in newspapers, then stirred two parts sugar into one part water in a heavy saucepan until it reached the soft-crack stage. He was humming to himself now, concentrating. He added a teaspoon of glucose, then continued to cook the mixture, stirring constantly until it had reached the hard-crack stage. Removing it from the burner, he set the pan momentarily in cold water to arrest the cooking, then back onto the still-warm stove. He came back to earth long enough to throw me an apologetic smile.

"Please shut the door so that neither the dogs nor Roger can come in," he said, and I grinned. Ah, yes. I could just picture one of the Pekinese covered in strands of sugar.

Placing an oiled broom handle between the center island and the countertop, he dipped a fork into the saucepan and twirled it, much as one does when eating spaghetti, until the tines were thick with the melted sugar. Then, in one fast, fluid movement, he pulled the fork from the pan and flicked it across the broom handle. The white-hot sugar flew from the fork, cooling instantaneously and forming long tendrils of cobwebby spun sugar.

Like an expert fencer drawing his épée, he repeated this operation until the section of broom handle was nearly invisible under the fine sugar filaments. Then, pulling them from the broom handle, he moulded the still-soft sugar strands over a tea cup into a lacy dome perhaps three inches in diameter. These finished confections would garnish a myriad of desserts ranging from crème brulée to baked alaska.

He turned to face me with a smile. *"Et voilà!"*

One of Marco's most charming mannerisms was his smile. When something turned out beautifully, though it always did—his face would light up with an excited, almost bashful grin, as if inviting you to marvel with him at the wonder of his success. A born teacher, he was always willing to share his knowledge to those who would listen. Often since, I've wished I had spent more time in the kitchen, learning from him how to create his fabulous dishes.

"Now, Christopher. You want the maximum volume

possible of egg whites when making meringues and soufflés," he'd say in a fatherly tone of voice, while I ironed the linens or polished silver. "That is why you bring eggs to room temperature by removing them from the refrigerator an hour before you need to use them. Do you see?"

I did see, but because I was young and couldn't be told anything, much of Marco's advice about life in general tended to go in one ear and out the other.

"Don't move around," he advised once. "Stay in one job and learn all you can. In this profession, longevity is the best thing you can show on your c.v."

In retrospect, it is my great regret that I didn't pay closer attention to his instructions. But I still consider it a rare and treasured opportunity to have been associated with him.

I appreciated Marco for another reason—he was one of the few people I could talk to in Switzerland. In my two summers there I met almost no one outside of his family and the odd supplier with whom we had business. On Sundays after lunch I drove into Lausanne to buy the English and American papers for Mr. and Mrs. Bristol. The newspaper shipment was scheduled to be delivered each week to the Lausanne train station, and they were very disappointed if it didn't arrive. I loved this errand. It was a break, a chance to get away, and other than on my day off, it was the only time I left the house. The relative isolation of the Maison des Fleurs left me little opportunity to meet other people; no village or pub was nearby. There was little to do except wander through the various counties (called cantons) and explore the pristine, picturesque villages. The scenery was beautiful, postcard perfect. But like a postcard, the people in the foreground might have been cardboard cutouts. I found the Swiss staid and unapproachable, and particularly to my young eyes, they certainly didn't seem to know how to have fun.

Thus it was I found myself driving back to Monte Carlo on my day off to spend a few hours with Deirdre or my mates from the boats. In the Mini, I could make the trip in just over five hours. But even taking the driving into consideration, I preferred the few short hours I'd spend in Monte Carlo. Otherwise my day off stretched long and lonely.

The second summer in Switzerland, I was wandering in Ouchy when I happened upon a small bar called the White Horse. But while the name reminded me of a pub in England, there the resemblance ended. No one who worked in it was English, but it was a bar where I stood a good chance of hearing the language spoken. And there I came to know Klaus, who became the one friend I made in Switzerland.

Klaus was in his early thirties, very tall with sandy blond hair and the well-defined physique of a swimmer. His broad smile was set into a square face whose complexion bespoke of long hours spent out-of-doors. In fact, he said, he owned a speed boat, from which he gave waterskiing lessons on Lake Geneva.

"A very fast boat," he said proudly in his German-accented English. "Many times I am asked by the wealthy businessmen to ferry them across to Evian, in France."

"Do you take them?" I asked.

He grinned. "Sometimes. But mostly, I say no, I can teach waterskiing and make more money. Then, perhaps, they pay more than I make to teach for one hour, and I take them."

"How much do you charge to learn to ski?" I was interested. This might be something I could take up to fill my free time.

"Three hundred Swiss francs an hour."

My face fell.

Smiling apologetically, he bought us both another drink.

If I thought I was bored on my day off, it was nothing to what Rosalie, Lady Welsh's granddaughter, felt when she came to visit for several weeks. She was not a happy guest. As a young person, she wasn't content to lounge by the pool and read, or play endless rubbers of bridge. Only eighteen years old, it seemed to her that she had been exiled to Switzerland, palmed off by her parents onto her grandparents. I felt immensely sorry for her. Knowing how frustrated she was, I tried hard to come up with ideas to entertain her.

"What do you do on your day off?" she asked me one day. "Aren't there any parties or anything to go to?"

"No parties that I've found, miss. I meet a friend of mine called Klaus for drinks at a bar in Ouchy."

"What's he like? What does he do?"

When I told her, there was a spark of interest in her dark eyes, the first I'd seen since she had arrived. "I'll ask my grandmother if I can learn to water ski," she said. "Will you talk to your friend?"

At the equivalent of $150 an hour, it was far more in her price range than it was in mine. I met with Klaus and explained the situation.

Klaus's ruddy face lit up. "Oh, yes? What does she look like?"

"Stop, she's only eighteen. Tall, long dark hair, a little pudgy. Tends to pout."

He laughed. "That is not surprising. Switzerland is known for being a winter destination for the young, not a summer one."

I had been thinking. "What about—if I bring her out for the afternoon next week, could you take me as well, at a reduced rate?"

He clapped me on the shoulder. "Christopher, bring her at the usual rate, and you shall learn too—no charge."

And so it was that, on a clear summer day in June, Rosalie and I learned to water ski in the icy blue waters of Lake Geneva. It was a wonderful afternoon. Klaus brought beer and I brought my camera. Rosalie was smiling and laughing for the first time since she had arrived. I was pleased to have succeeded in finding her a happy diversion, and even more so that I had been able to enjoy it as well.

"Thank you, Christopher," she said with a wide smile, as I dropped her at the front door before garaging the car. "That was the most fun I've had all summer."

Still, it was with great relief that I packed the Buick for the household's return to Monte Carlo for the winter season. I greeted Rudy and Cosimo, the gardener, like long-lost friends. And there was another friendly face; because the daily cleaner had moved away, I was able to recommend that Cassie, who had once endorsed me as a steward on the *Serendipity,* take her place.

Lady Welsh rented the Villa San Felipe in Villefranche-sur-Mer, a house she continued to rent for the rest of the time I was with her. A spectacular residence set high into the cliffs overlooking the sea, the Villa San Felipe was reached from the Moyenne Corniche—one of the Côte d'Azur's primary roads—which ran above it, by descending a steep driveway with a hairpin bend midway. At the curve, a three-car garage with adjoining staff quarters was set into the side of the cliff. The drive terminated in a wide circular courtyard in which a small grove of olive trees was planted.

A massive grand entrance, complete with tall, arched wooden doors adorned the castle-like facade. The house was built almost entirely of rough-hewn stone and was replete with terraces, turrets, and arched windows framed by operative white shutters. The main house had two floors and three bedrooms; three detached guest suites were built into the hill under the car park level.

Best of all, the Villa San Felipe had an entirely separate gatehouse at the top of the drive, right off the Moyenne Corniche, which was assigned to me. It had a fully equipped kitchen, a double bed, and its own garage, where I kept the Mini (which I had bought from Lady Welsh when she had decided to trade it in for a Volkswagen GTI). The gatehouse, as staff quarters, surpassed my wildest dreams. After working hours, I could come and go unnoticed, and I had somewhere I could entertain friends without fearing reprisal from my employers. I wondered if Mr. Bristol, remembering my disgrace that first New Year's Eve, had suggested the housing arrangement.

The following winter the South of France had a bizarre severe snowstorm, the first time in over a hundred years that snow had settled. The one overworked snowplow, usually at the Nice Airport, went up and down the Basse Corniche and the Moyenne Corniche, trying to restore order to the disorientated communities.

Lady Welsh was a panic buyer. As the snowstorm continued, she insisted that Rudy and I go out and buy all the meat, vegetables, and groceries we could get in the shops. The pair of us struggled out into the driving snow and motored into the village, the little Volkswagen GTI sliding on the roads. We were unhappy with her request, not because we had to brave the weather, but because we feared it was a poor public relations move. And our fears were well founded. We were booed and hissed at in the boucherie by the local people, who were buying the one small piece of meat they could afford.

Mr. and Mrs. Bristol had been invited to a dinner party that night at the Hôtel Hermitage in Monte Carlo. In spite of the icy, hazardous driving conditions, she wouldn't hear of not attending the party. Therefore, although dinner wasn't until half past seven, we started out at a little after five for a destination that under normal circumstances would have taken less than twenty minutes to travel.

The driveway was thick with ice. I knew there wasn't any way to maneuver the car down to the front door and collect them, then attempt to scale the steep hairpin driveway, so Rudy and I came up with a plan. The servant's entrance next to the garage was nearest the road. We decided to bring Lady Welsh up from there to the top of the driveway, where I had left the heavy Rolls Royce, warm and running, at the gatehouse. To melt the ice and give us traction, Rudy threw boxes of salt on the stairs from the servant's entrance to the top. Then, very solicitous, he, Mr. Bristol, Isobel, and I all helped Lady Welsh heave her fur-encased bulk up the stairs and into the waiting car. The laborious process took us nearly fifteen minutes.

My windscreen wipers swiped vainly as snow whipped from every direction. There was hardly any traffic; sensible people knew it was foolish to drive in such weather.

Until we reached Eze, the road was very flat, but then it began to climb. Ahead of us, I saw some well-dressed younger people who were trying to get their BMW up the hill. In order to get some traction, they had taken the car mats out of the car and wedged them under the wheels.

From the back seat, Lady Welsh saw this, too. "Take the lower road, the one which skirts the village," she instructed.

It was getting very, very dark as we came across a line of stationary cars in the right-hand lane of the dual carriageway. Everyone had stopped, obviously waiting for something.

"Take the left-hand lane," she ordered.

"But madame—"

"I do *not* want to be late for the dinner."

This maneuver caused quite a furor among the drivers of the other cars. Through the windscreen I could hear their boos and hisses. "Get back in this lane!" they called indignantly as we passed by in the big car.

Within a few minutes we came upon the accident that was the cause of the delay, and slowly, very gingerly, I braked and we came to a gradual stop.

A policeman dispatched himself from the fray, not at all pleased to find us in the left-hand lane where they were trying to clear the accident. "Get in the other lane, and do it smartly," he ordered angrily.

As he strode away, he slipped on the pervasive black ice—the cause of the accident in the first place—and fell on his *derrière.* His weight as he hit the road caused enough of a vibration that our two-and-a-half ton car (independent of its occupants) slid ninety degrees into the center divider.

Fortunately, up against the divider we had some traction, so I was able to coax the Rolls to creep round the bend. Even so, we made it to l'Hermitage at 8:15 P.M.—forty-five minutes late for dinner. And she was angry at me because of it.

We drove home late that night without incident—until we reached the house, when we were faced with the enormous drop in the driveway with the hairpin bend midway down. And this time Lady Welsh wouldn't hear of being escorted down to the service entrance, the way we'd taken her up. "No," she said peremptorily. "You are going to drive down and let me off at the front door."

"But Mrs. Bristol—"

"Do. As. I. Say."

As I pulled into the entrance to the drive, I could see Rudy with the salt and the broom, preparing the area to which he thought she would come. His face looking up at us turned incredulous when he saw me start down the drive.

I tried to creep down that hill, but by the time we got to the hairpin bend we were doing 15–20 mph with next to no traction. Luckily I just got steerage going round the bend. But the momentum sent the heavy Rolls fish-tailing round the hairpin turn, and it continued to spin, doing a 360-degree turn on the icy driveway.

What seemed to me like ages later, we stopped spinning, and I wordlessly brought the car slowly to the front door. Rudy and Isobel had hurried over and were waiting to help Lady Welsh from the car.

As soon as the front door closed on her, Rudy turned to me, screaming. "What you think you doing, bringing that expensive car down that hill!" I couldn't answer. My insides were still shaking from the slide. Needless to say, I left the Rolls in the courtyard that night.

But the next day, as I served morning coffee, Lady Welsh spoke to me.

"You did well, driving the car to the front door last night. Thank you," she said with a nod. "I think you deserve to know why I was so insistent that you do so.

"Some years ago, I had one of my hips replaced. The operation was botched by the surgeon, and evidence I found later makes me suspect him of being drunk during the operation. In any event it has, for me, been a very painful mistake.

"Last night's conditions made me afraid of a fall that might require another operation, which I cannot risk. The car costs perhaps £80,000, and I can replace it if necessary. But I cannot replace my hip."

It was the most personal admission I ever heard from her.

Private service is not a profession for people who need a lot of praise; rather, the opposite is true. If a servant does his job faultlessly, he is invisible; if imperfectly, he is noticed and perhaps reprimanded. I had learned a great deal about being unobtrusive through service in restaurants and aboard the yachts, now I worked to perfect it.

In the absence of recognition, I garnered pleasure in endeavoring to do my job flawlessly. I took pains with my appearance, making sure my shirts were immaculate and starched to perfection, my trousers free of lint and pressed with military-like creases, my hair neatly cut, my fingernails short and always impeccably clean. I absorbed Lady Welsh's and Mr. Bristol's habits so that I could anticipate their wants and needs. It became a point of pride to me if I got through a day without being asked for something that I hadn't anticipated. In an effort to bring diversity to an often repetitive job, I served my employers on different-patterned china plates each day, and varied the types of flowers that graced the tables often. On the rare occasions when I was able to observe one of my peers on duty, I took pains to note and duplicate his actions and mannerisms. I aspired to a level of service so perfect, it would seem almost as if I weren't there.

This is not to say that a butler should go wholly unnoticed. I learned it was appropriate to make enough of an impression on guests that they remembered and thought well of you. I was pleased when Mr. and Mrs. Bristol's guests would greet me by name and add perhaps a word or two. But, as was proper, I never extended the conversation beyond a query as to their health or something equally inconsequential. While a butler might come to know a fair amount about frequent visitors, a comment such as "I trust, Sir Quentin, that you accomplished the buyout of XYZ Corporation successfully?" would be considered impertinent. Employers and guests choose to believe that butlers, though omnipresent, are deaf to their conversations, no matter how interesting they might be.

When Lady Welsh attended social events held in private households, I'd be invited in to sit with their servants in the staff room. Initially this prospect had interested me, as I looked forward to meeting others in the trade, but I was soon disappointed with the results. Without exception, every other butler, chef, or chauffeur I ever met was my senior by thirty-five years, and had been in service his entire life. Most, in fact, had been in the same household since they had been children. And, far from it being an opportunity to talk, to exchange ideas and information, they saw these visits only as a chance for an evening in front of the television. The only conversation I could elicit about the job was a litany of complaints that all fell under the heading "Back in the Good Old Days When We Had Proper Staff, Such-and-Such Never Would Have Happened." Did they know of anyone my age to whom I could speak? I would ask. No, they'd say. Nobody's going into service anymore. The jobs are disappearing.

Yes, it was obvious that the old servant class was, literally, dying out. True, money and other factors had taken their toll on the large households in which these servants were brought up; even the old-school wealthy had less staff than had their parents. But while the writing was on the wall, I chose to interpret it differently.

For the first time, I began to see a future in what I was doing; a career, rather than just a job. The problem, as I saw it, was that these domestic employees saw their positions as being strictly differentiated, and were unwilling to change or expand their skill base. But even if the staff levels in the large estates continued to dwindle, surely there was a market for someone who was willing to do more than just one narrowly defined job. These upper-class employers had children who had been brought up with household staff, yet there was no influx of younger servants to attend their households. Why not be a big fish in a little pond, instead of the other way round? The more I could do, the more indispensable I might become. And if there were this few of us in the trade, I might have a profession for life.

One Christmas—my third with Lady Welsh—Marco came to the Côte d'Azur for the holiday week. He was relieving Rudy so that the latter could spend it with his family in London, and had brought, with Lady Welsh's permission, his wife and two teenage children.

We arranged to have a staff Christmas dinner for Christmas Eve, after The Receiving of the Gift ceremony in Lady Welsh's drawing room. There were nine of us, for in addition to Marco and his family, Isobel, and myself, Cassie had brought her husband, and there was a daily houseman named Richard, who worked as an under-butler when needed. I'd used him that night, since their traditional Christmas Eve supper required a lot of side dishes that needed to be passed.

One of the nice things about the Villa San Felipe was that the staff room was quite a distance from the rest of the living quarters, so we didn't feel we always had to speak in low voices. It was a convivial evening, probably the best time I ever had with everyone there. It was a rare occasion to be a staff united. Isobel and Cassie had decorated the staff room in festive reds and greens. Richard had set the staff table, and I had found traditional English Christmas crackers to adorn each plate. And Marco had created a meal that eclipsed, I thought, the more conventional meal I had just served to Lady Welsh and her ten guests. Noteworthy among the courses was an elaborate salmon mousse shaped and decorated like a fish. He had painted the mould with aspic just on the verge of setting, then layered into it thinly sliced cucumbers, which formed the scales. A slice of pimento-stuffed olive was used for the fish's eye, and the body cavity was filled with caviar. To say it was far more grand than our usual fare is quite an understatement.

After dinner we exchanged small gifts, each from our own perspective or field of expertise. Isobel had embroidered for each of us our monogram on fine linen handkerchiefs while Marco had created individual *gateaux*. I gave everyone a bottle of wine to which I'd tied a Cadbury's Flake chocolate bar. Roger the parrot napped in the corner of the room during the party. We'd bought him his very own box of McVitie's Chocolate Biscuits, and there was a discarded pile of naked shortbread on the floor under his perch.

Marco's presence, though pleasant, acted as a reminder to

me that in a few short months, we would be heading back to Switzerland. For several weeks there had been a gnawing sensation in my gut over the decision I dreaded making—whether or not to stay with Lady Welsh in this position. I had already spoken a little to Rudy about my dilemma. Yes, it was a steady job, but I emphatically did not want to return to Switzerland in the spring. I didn't mind working the long days, but I wanted to stay in a locale where I had some opportunity for a life in my off-hours. Bloody hell, I was only twenty-six years old. Going to Switzerland was like being entombed.

And I was resentful—I had only received that one £5 per week rise in the two and one-half years I'd been with Lady Welsh. Regardless of how well one did, there were no Christmas bonuses, and her lack of interest was evident in her choice of gifts. (It had been another sweater year, fuchsia this time.)

I told Marco about my quandary on Christmas Eve. I had splurged on a bottle of port, and after the others had retired, he and I shared a nightcap back at my gatehouse.

Predictably, he was fatherly in his guidance. "Stay with it," he advised. "It's better for your career in the long term if you've got at least five years in one place. And you'll meet more people in Switzerland as time goes by."

And as usual, I didn't pay attention.

The day I informed Lady Welsh of my decision to resign was one of the worst of my life. I had prepared my speech, and, moreover, I had taken pains to sound out Richard as a possible replacement, so that I had a successor ready to suggest. I expected it was a matter of complete indifference to her who did my job, as long as someone was doing it, and correctly. They seemed to like Richard, and so I had spent some time training him to their standards.

I approached her after tea, when Mr. Bristol was out with the dogs.

"Excuse me, Mrs. Bristol?"

She didn't look up from her book, assuming, I suppose, that I merely wanted to take something out of her way. I had said so little to her over the course of my employment that I wasn't sure she'd have recognized my voice. I tried again.

"If I might have a word, Mrs. Bristol."

"Yes, what is it?" She set her book aside a little crossly.

My practiced speech poured out in a straight line, without punctuation. "I should like to give you notice that I wish to leave—I realize that my leaving might prove a hardship so I propose to give two months' notice—I have taken the liberty of ascertaining that Richard, whom you've met, may be available to assume my position—Would you give me a reference please as I intend to continue in this line of work—"

"What?!"

I cannot remember the exact words she hurled at me, but of her feelings I had no doubt. She was offended, considering it an audacity, a betrayal that I would consider leaving.

I was at a loss for words. I couldn't believe it. I didn't know what else to say. I felt I'd done my homework, finding her someone who wanted the job, someone I could train easily.

But though she was outraged that I would want to go, she never once asked why.

The last week I was there was pretty frosty. Lady Welsh did allow me, very reluctantly, to bring Richard in a couple of times to see the routine, though she was still trying to get me to change my mind. In the meantime, I had no job to go to, so money was paramount in my mind. I had spoken to Roy, the owner of the Bar des Anglais, and arranged to be a temporary barman for him in a few weeks' time. Deirdre and I had split up, but a friend offered me her couch to sleep on until I could afford a place of my own. My next month's mortgage on the English house was due in three weeks. I had been allocating every last penny from my final paycheck.

On my last day she handed me my paycheck in an envelope with, unfairly, the barest of references. I looked at the check and my heart sank. It did not have the accumulated two weeks' holiday pay that was due me. With trepidation, I went back into her study—even though she had closed the door—to question her about it.

"I'm sorry, Mrs. Bristol, but there seems to be a mistake. I'm due two weeks' holiday, which doesn't seem to appear on this check," I said.

Her multiple chins came up defiantly. "You are leaving me after *only* two and one-half years," she said haughtily. "We taught you everything you know. I am *not* going to pay you for your holiday."

I was furious, but I kept my voice even. "Mrs. Bristol, that is against the law and highly immoral. I've earned that money. I've given you sufficient notice, and have found and trained my replacement. I could have taken the time off in lieu of payment, but instead chose to work to the end to make it as easy as possible for you. I am entitled to that money."

It was the most I had ever said to her. Her eyebrows rose, and it was obvious she was surprised that I would stand up to her. This was not the subservient servant that she'd thought me to be.

Although I was very intimidated by her, I was backed into a corner. I had to have that money to live on in the next two weeks before I could start at the Bar des Anglais. I had no work visa in France.

I'm not proud of it, but with no recourse, I fought back the only way I could think of. Although my stomach was shaking, I tried to put steel in my voice. "If you don't pay me what I'm due, I will get you where it hurts."

"What *are* you talking about?"

"Your dogs," I whispered. It was an empty threat, but she'd never known me well enough to know it.

There was absolute silence. Confusion—why isn't this person going away like he's supposed to?—was replaced by horror on her face. Then the folds in her neck began to quiver and her chest heaved angrily.

"How *dare* you," she bellowed, her face deep red. "Get *out* of my sight. Leave this *instant*." Turning on her heel, she snatched up Pippa, who happened to be the closest, and did her best to stalk out of the room. The rest of the Pekinese, interested in this unusual exchange but thankfully ignorant of its contents, trotted out of the room at her heels, with a backward look at me.

I went to Rudy in a near panic and told him what I'd said. "Rudy, I need that money. I've earned that money. You know I'd never hurt the dogs, but I didn't know what else to say. I felt powerless to fight her in any other way. What can I do?"

Rudy poured me a tot of brandy and squeezed my shoulder. "Just sit there. I will be back in a short while."

I learned later that he spoke to Isobel, then Cassie, then went to Lady Welsh.

"He has earned that money, madame," he told her. "If you do not pay him what is earned, which is illegal, then we—Isobel, Cassie, and I—shall leave as well."

In the end she wrote out the check. Rudy brought it to me. "You had best leave now," he said. Grabbing me in a bear hug, he kissed both my cheeks in the French fashion.

"Good luck, my friend." He smiled, though his eyes were moist. *"Buona fortuna."*

I closed the door quietly behind me.

# 8

# The Urban Cowboy

"Chris! Come down here, mate, I've got something for you," Geoff waved to me from the end of the bar.

Geoff was captain of the yacht *Nemesis,* and I had been in touch with him on and off since my days as a steward. After sliding the pint of lager to my customer, I came over to see what he was on about.

"I met an American in the gym at Loews the other day," he said, referring to one of the famous Monte Carlo casinos. "He needs a butler, and I told him you might be interested. Are you still looking for a house job?"

I was. "An American? What do you know about him?"

"All I know is that his name is Carstairs and he's a businessman from California. Big guy. Looks like a cowboy. He could be straight out of a John Wayne movie. He's rented the Maison du Gouverneur for the season."

I whistled, intrigued. Now one of the largest estates in the medieval village of Roquebrune, the Maison du Gouverneur had, as its name suggested, originally been the residence of the governor when the town was a separately administered village. Renting it would not have been cheap.

"Who's there now?" I asked him, referring to the staff.

"That's the rub—no one, other than a daily housekeeper. It's a good story; he'll tell you about it. I'll see him at Loews tomorrow evening. When can you meet him?" We arranged an interview for two days hence at a beachside café.

Arriving at the appointed location, I had no difficulty in identifying Mr. Carstairs. Geoff wasn't joking about his looking like a cowboy; he looked like a cross between Sean Connery and the Marlboro Man. His thinning chestnut brown hair was liberally streaked by the sun with gold, and he wore a jaunty well-trimmed beard and moustache. Easily six foot four, bronzed, and well muscled, only the slight crow's feet around his light eyes gave away his middle age. I approached him and introduced myself.

"Jack Carstairs," he said with a grin that displayed perfect white teeth.

I'm sure the contrast between us as we shook hands was extreme. In addition to the foot-plus difference in height, I had dressed in a dark coat and tie appropriate to the position of butler. Mr. Carstairs wore white linen trousers, and his light sports shirt was open at the neck, exposing a mat of dark chest hair set off by a gold chain.

"I've rented this place in Roquebrune," he said, as we sat down and ordered cappuccinos. "I originally had a couple in there, but right now I'm stuck." The story he told was something that could only happen in France.

The Maison du Gouverneur had come staffed with an old French couple named Marie and Pierre, who, Mr. Carstairs was told, had been there for years. But, unfortunately, shortly after he had arrived, Marie had died. Pierre took a few days off to take care of the funeral arrangements, but had returned within the week.

"He was there for about three days, but he was a wreck. I'd ask for a meal and get it two hours later, burned to a crisp. Things were forgotten. The whole place was a disaster.

"I felt bad for the man," Mr. Carstairs said. "I figured he

hadn't had time to really get himself together after the death of his wife. So I gave him two weeks' bereavement leave."

After the allotted two weeks, Pierre had returned, and Mr. Carstairs had greeted him with the news that he was expecting a houseful of company by the end of the week. But the day his visitors were to arrive, Pierre came in to work with a note from his doctor stating that he was under severe mental stress and required ten days' leave.

"I was stuck, but what could I do? I took my guests out for dinner every night, or the housekeeper made up some simple meals that we could reheat.

"Anyway, after the ten days were up, the guy came back. I had invited six people for dinner on Friday. The following day, Thursday, he came back with another note requiring an additional forty-five days off!"

He took a drink of his cappuccino before he continued. "I could see the writing on the wall. This was some sort of a scam—he would continue to come back with notes, and there wasn't anything I could do about it. And then I was talking to that guy Geoff and he knew all about it. Must be a small town."

Geoff, Mr. Carstairs said, knew of the caretakers, and knew Pierre hadn't contributed much to the job he and his wife had jointly held—Marie had done all of the cooking and shopping, while he had only served the meals. But unwilling to give up the fairly cushy position after the death of his wife, Pierre had tried to fake it. Whenever Mr. Carstairs asked for a meal, Pierre would run up the hill to the local café to ask the landlady how to prepare it. But he couldn't cook, and his attempts to do so had been disastrous. Faced with possible exposure, he looked for another way out.

The French social system is such that a doctor's note can legitimately excuse one from work indefinitely. Pierre, it turned out, had a good friend who was a doctor, and this friend had been issuing his notes.

"So I just paid the guy for the forty-five days and told him I wouldn't require his services at the end of it. Let's see if he has the balls to come back and tell me I can't fire him." He took a long drink and looked at me. "So that's why I need someone, and Geoff said you're good."

I gave him my c.v. and my references, including Lady Welsh's sketchy referral, and outlined my experience. He seemed pleased with the breadth of my background.

He wanted, he said, someone to manage the house and deal with the live-out staff; someone who could cook decent meals and serve them; someone who could handle his French correspondence and act as a translator. "But it would only be until September, when I go back to California. Are you willing to take a six-month position?"

Butler, chef, translator, personal secretary . . . this was certainly closer to what I had in mind, even if it was short-term. "Yes, sir."

"Good. Can you start tomorrow?"

"I'm afraid not, sir." I knew instinctively this was a man used to getting his own way. "I'd like to, but I owe it to Roy to cover my scheduled shifts so he isn't stuck. Will one week from today be satisfactory?"

He was somewhat disappointed, but said he appreciated my integrity. We negotiated a salary that took into account the increase in my responsibilities over those at my last household. It wasn't a princely sum, but it was still quite a bit more than Lady Welsh had paid me. With a casual wave, my new boss departed.

As an employer, Mr. Carstairs was unlike anyone I'd ever encountered before. For a start, I had thought it odd when he told me to report for work my first day at "around ten" in the morning. But having done so, when I asked the amiable housekeeper, Mathilde, where I might find him, her fleshy face creased into a merry smile.

"Monsieur? Ach, he isn't yet awake," she said. "He will not appear until nearly midday. Come, I will show you around."

Perched 250 feet up steep reddish-brown cliffs overlooking Menton and the Monte Carlo harbor, the Maison du Gouverneur was truly something to see. Its fifty-four rooms featured painted frescoes on the walls, while windows and balconies everywhere captured the phenomenal view below. At least a dozen guest rooms faced the sea opening off long internal corridors, while the medium-sized kitchen and various other service rooms were built up against the cliff side. One of these interior rooms, set back into the hill, was currently functioning as a wine cellar. Stacked cases of good red wine lined the windowless room.

Acres of immaculate terraced gardens were contained within the stone wall around and below the Maison du Gouverneur. Stone balustrades surrounded the pristine white gravel paths that led through such delights as a rose garden, a formal French garden with topiary hedges and symmetrical ornamental trees, a flagstone-bordered koi pond replete with lily pads and burbling fountain and a sun garden set off by a large bronze sun sculpture. A bougainvillaea-covered arbor past the koi pond led out to Inspiration Point, where benches and railings enclosed a semicircular lookout area. The view encompassed the stepped plateaus of fruit trees in the foreground, and the Grimaldi castle in Monaco beyond. One sixty-six-year-old gardener named Prudeup tended all the grounds alone. Not surprisingly, he was wiry and muscular, incredibly fit.

The villa could only be reached on foot from a steep stairway that ran alongside it between the Basse Corniche, at beach level, to the Place Ingram, in the center of the ancient fortified *castellum* of Roquebrune. Only one road allowed access to the village, and no cars were permitted beyond the village square; its medieval streets consisted of a labyrinth of narrow, twisted passageways over which loomed houses chiseled out of the rock of the old fortress. The estate's three-car garage was located on the Basse Corniche from which one could count on a seven to eight minute hike up the stairway to the house.

My quarters consisted of a two-room apartment at the back of the sun garden, with a separate entrance off the staircase. It wasn't as posh as my gatehouse had been at the Villa San Felipe, but I knew the latter had been the exception rather than the rule. What was convenient was its proximity—just up the stairway—to the village and its cafés, which were the local watering holes.

Everything about working for Mr. Carstairs was a study in contrasts. Although I wore the same uniform as ever—white shirt, black trousers, and tie—during the day, he had tuxedos custom-made for me to wear when he entertained. It was a far cry from Lady Welsh's hand-me-down white jacket.

On my first day he pulled his wallet out and handed me 3,000 francs. "There you go," he said, putting the wallet back in his pocket. "Let me know when you need more." True, I was responsible for buying everything for the house, including the food, not just petrol and incidentals. Still, I was astonished and gratified at this show of trust.

One thing that was immediately apparent was that Mr. Carstairs had not been brought up in households with domestic staff, nor had he ever employed them, except for occasional cleaning help. One of the first mornings I was with him, after I had checked on his plans for dinner and was preparing to go, he suddenly began to talk. I had become so used to being invisible in Lady Welsh's employ that I was unprepared for Mr. Carstairs' breezy openness.

"You see, one of the main reasons I hired you is that I don't have a wife right now to arrange for everything, and I need someone to look after me," he said. As he seemed to want a response, I mumbled something noncommittal. I had never thought about being compared to a wife. "In fact, I'm here because my wife wants a divorce, and she wanted some space."

I was surprised, not only that he would make me privy to such information after so short an acquaintance, but in his delivery of it. I couldn't see a trace of anxiety or concern on his rugged, suntanned face.

"I'm sorry, sir," I murmured.

"Oh, I don't know if I am. I guess it had to come out someday. See, she found out that I had been having an affair for the past ten years."

I didn't know what to say to such a revelation, so rather inanely, I repeated my apology.

"Yeah, so she wants time on her own to decide what to do."

"I see, sir."

"I'm supposed to be deciding what I want to do, too. But in the meantime, I found this place, and I'm gonna enjoy myself. Life is too short, right?"

"Yes, sir. Uh . . . will that be all, sir?"

His lifestyle, as well, was a far cry from that which I had left. Whatever his feelings about his potential divorce, it was evident that Mr. Carstairs was taking the cliché "sun, sea, sand, and sex" image of the Côte d'Azur very seriously indeed. Since his arrival, he'd taken advantage of an opportunity to purchase a two-bedroom high-rise apartment in Monte Carlo, so that he could walk to the beach. However, the beaches in Monte Carlo are private; those with sufficient capital may rent a spot on the beach for the season. Since he always had a retinue of family or friends around him, Mr. Carstairs had rented eight or ten spots.

As Mathilde had said, he would get up about noon, and have a light breakfast, usually only coffee, fruit juice, and lots of milk over ice. After breakfast, he would drive his Ferrari down to his flat, and from there go to the beach. There he would work on his tan and "check out the girls" until four or five o'clock, then go to the gym at Loews Casino for a workout. Coming back to Roquebrune, he'd take a siesta until perhaps 7 P.M., after which, if he wasn't dining elsewhere or going to a show, he might have cocktails and perhaps a few people in for dinner.

Once I had cleaned up the kitchen after dinner, I would be off for the evening, after which I could take my Mini into Monte Carlo, or walk up into Roquebrune. As the nightlife doesn't start in the South of France until midnight, the timing was ideal.

As for Mr. Carstairs, it was not unusual for him to take a swim in the pool at 1:30 A.M., then go into Monte Carlo, where there was a big club scene, to go dancing until the wee hours of the morning.

The pace was fast, exciting—particularly after my service with Mr. and Mrs. Bristol. This man *lived* his life. Always, there were things to do, people to see, arrangements to make. It was my job to take over the mundane necessities of Mr. Carstairs's life, leaving him free to do what he wanted. He wasn't the sort who would generally plan things far in advance; rather, he preferred to throw unexpected situations at me, then see if I could handle it.

"Chris, I'd like dinner for twelve tomorrow."

"Fine, sir. What sort of food would you like?"

"I don't know. You choose." Not only was such a directive challenging, it was exhilarating. I had never had such freedom in my job.

Mr. Carstairs liked to entertain at the big house, and most nights he would have people to dinner. In the European custom, these dinner parties would start late, often seating at 9:30 P.M. Of interest to me were the people Mr. Carstairs invited. They were hardly those likely to grace Lady Welsh's table. Most of his guests were younger, lively people: other Americans on holiday, pit-bosses and show girls from Loews Casino. One and all, they seemed to have an uproariously good time.

They rarely ate at the dining table inside, preferring to enjoy the balmy Mediterranean night air and spectacular view of Monte Carlo on the balcony outside. Although to Mr. Carstairs, any excuse for a party was a good one, Prince Rainier's fireworks competition in late July provided a better reason that most. The annual event drew participants from all over the world who shot off impressive pyrotechnic displays from barges in the harbor. The shows were synchronized to music, which we were too far away to hear, but for several nights the presentations provided magnificent dinner entertainment.

In addition to local guests, friends of Mr. Carstairs and his family from the States came out for a couple of weeks at a time. Certainly, with a house the size of the Maison du Gouverneur, space was not a problem. These spirited visitors were definitely on holiday, and they enjoyed themselves. At noon, guests would wander in for breakfast, usually hung over from the previous night's entertainment. In addition to the buffet-style meal I'd have laid, pitchers of Bloody Marys were *de rigueur.*

Life was very different in Roquebrune. The shops, cafés, and restaurants were geared towards tourists. Because a bakery and a delicatessen were the only purveyors of foodstuffs, I drove the Ferrari to Menton or Monte Carlo to shop for provisions. The fact that I already knew the territory was to my advantage, as I didn't have to establish new contacts for good meat, seafood, vegetables, bread, etc. I had been on the Côte d'Azur long enough to know who the better chefs used and recommended. But since no cars were allowed in the village, bringing the groceries back was tricky. I could park either in the town square and walk through a quarter-mile of alleyways to the staircase, then down forty feet of steps, or I could park in the garage on the Basse Corniche, walk a block to the staircase, then straight up the hill to the estate. In the perched village, either way involved lots of steps. It was no wonder Prudeup was in great shape.

There were no animals to feed, and the capable Mathilde handled all the cleaning, including what little silver there was. Primarily, I shopped for and cooked the meals and served them. I rarely knew how many people were expected for dinner. Mr. Carstairs' directive was that I always have something in the refrigerator ready to go on a few hours' notice, saying he would prefer to throw something out because it had spoiled than to be caught short.

With only a very few caveats—such as no fried foods—he allowed me to choose the menus, and was appreciative of the results. He liked "healthy, tasty food," meaning lots of fresh fish, vegetables, and fruits. It was my introduction to something I learned later was indicative of "California cuisine."

I had been with him less than a week and was finalizing the clean-up of the kitchen after dinner when Mr. Carstairs came in and sat down at the staff table. It had, I was to find

## An Easy, Elegant Starter Course
## Avocado Marie Rose

*Serves 8*

4 avocados
½ lb. tiny bay shrimp, cooked
¼ cup white wine vinegar (or any flavored vinegar)
lemon juice
cayenne pepper or paprika
flat parsley, lemon wedges, and curly red lettuce for garnish

*Marie Rose Sauce*

4 tbsp. mayonnaise
3 tbsp. ketchup
1 tsp. horseradish
Tabasco
Worcestershire sauce
1 tsp. Pernod or scotch (optional)

Using ripe avocados (they should be quite soft, but not mushy), halve them lengthwise and remove seeds. Cut a small slice out of skin so that the avocado half sits flat on plate, cut side up. Sprinkle with lemon juice to prevent it from darkening.

Marinate the bay shrimp for fifteen minutes in white wine vinegar to which a few dashes of Tabasco has been added. Drain and chill until composing the starter.

Make the Marie Rose sauce: Mix mayonnaise, ketchup, and horseradish until well mixed. Add a dash of Worcestershire sauce and Tabasco to taste. The liquor, if you're using it, should be added at this point as well. (The French like Pernod, but I prefer to omit the liquor.)

Pile chilled bay shrimp in the seed cavity of the prepared avocado and top with a generous tablespoon of Marie Rose sauce. Sprinkle with a tiny amount of cayenne pepper or paprika to taste. Garnish with a sprig of flat parsley and serve on a leaf of curly red lettuce leaf and a wedge of lemon.

out, been one of the rare occasions that he dined alone. He carried a bottle of cognac and two brandy snifters in one hand.

"Here, Chris, pull up a chair," he said, indicating the one opposite.

"Sir?"

"Have a seat." I sat down hesitantly. He held up the bottle invitingly. "Drink?"

"Oh no, sir. Thank you anyway."

"Oh, come on, I insist." He poured two hefty snifters and held his up in a salute. "I think we should get to know each other a little better. Great dinner tonight, by the way. Cheers." He drank.

I took a small sip. The mellow cognac slid down my throat like a warm blanket, though I was acutely aware that sharing a drink with one's employer wasn't on the recommended deportment list for butlers.

"I think you do a fine job," he said. "You seem to know what you're doing, and how to handle everybody."

"Thank you, sir." This was more praise than I'd received from anyone. Maybe having a drink with one's employer wasn't such a bad idea.

"How would you like to run my estate in California?"

Go to *California*? YEE HAH! Lights, bells, and whistles went off in my head, although my face showed only a small smile. I had set a private goal to make it to the States by the time I was thirty. "I would be honored, sir."

At his insistence, we moved out to the balcony where, for several hours, he continued to pour cognac into both of our glasses as he talked about everything under the sun. He was trying to see what I was made of, I suspected, by getting me drunk. But I had spent several years working on the boats, where the ability to drink heavily yet hold one's alcohol is a necessity. And I feared that disgracing myself would somehow eliminate the California offer. After the bottle of cognac was finished, I returned the compliment by introducing him to vintage port, then had to put him to bed.

Guarding against familiarity is one of the most complex aspects of private service, and I could see that with an employer like Mr. Carstairs that this was going to prove more difficult than usual. I would not recommend this behavior to other butlers, but it certainly cemented our relationship.

For the most part, Mr. Carstairs' dinner guests were people just passing through on holiday. He didn't seem to know many other Côte d'Azur residents. This was largely due, I suspected, to the fact that he spoke no French. One of my jobs was to act as translator between him and the gardener and housekeeper, and he had begun to take me along to tailors and the like to interpret for him.

He was on his own one night, his most recent batch of visitors from the States having left. I had previously asked for the evening off to attend the monthly meeting of the English Club; and the more I considered it, the more I wondered if Mr. Carstairs might not enjoy meeting some other English-speaking people.

The English Club was a loosely run organization that existed only to provide an outlet for meeting other people who spoke English. There were no membership requirements or dues; it wasn't even necessary that English be one's first language. A fixed-price dinner meeting was held once a month at a local restaurant. Attendees, who included natives of Italy, the Sudan, Australia, and Africa, usually lived in the South of France for business reasons, and the only thing they had in common was the English language.

"Perhaps you might like to come?" I suggested, as I prepared a salad to leave in the refrigerator for his dinner. He was interested and, after getting directions to the restaurant, ambled off to change.

I had arranged to pick up someone else, so we took separate cars and met at the door, where he insisted on paying for my ticket. He disappeared into the crowd at the bar, and soon I saw him chatting with Texas Tamara, who I knew to be a show-girl at Loews Casino.

The English Club dinners were set up at long tables seating twenty or more. Although we were seated at different tables, I was glad to see that Mr. Carstairs was enjoying himself. In fact, as the evening progressed, it was clear that he was having a roaring good time. He was the life and soul of the party. He had arranged to sponsor the bar tab and was buying everyone snifters of Grand Marnier, Tia Maria, and Sambuca. Needless to say, the substantial crowd around him was also having a great time.

About 12:30 A.M. the party began to break up into smaller groups and head off to other nightlife activities. But Mr. Carstairs wasn't the sort to be a follower.

I was on my way out when I heard him corral the group. He was talking excitedly. "No, I have a better idea; let's go to my house!" He looked over their heads and caught sight of me trying to sneak away. "Oh Chris, hang on a minute!"

I looked back, dismayed. There he was, surrounded by this crowd of people, beckoning to me. I approached reluctantly.

"Everybody, this is Chris!" he said expansively. "He's my butler! He'll prepare us all breakfast!"

Oh, *shit!*

I tore out of the parking lot and drove like crazy to do whatever preparation I could before the crowd descended on me. Parking the Mini in the village square, I dashed into the closest bar/café and accosted Michel, the owner, who was behind the bar.

"I need a favor," I panted.

"No drinks on credit," he said.

"No, I need food. My boss has just invited forty people back for breakfast. Can I raid the fridge?"

His eyebrows went up, and he grinned. "Be my guest, as long as you replace it first thing tomorrow. What do you want?"

"Everything," I told him.

There was a slight pause, then with typical French aplomb, Michel laughed. "Eh, what the hell, maybe we won't serve food tomorrow. *C'est la vie*!"

From his larder, I took every egg, bottle of milk and cream, piece of cheese, meat, bread and salami I could lay hands on. Back at the house I made a vat of coffee and, as the people began streaming into the Maison du Gouverneur, began preparing a special coffee drink with Drambuie. By the number of coffees mixed, I learned that forty-two people had accepted Mr. Carstairs' offer. They were everywhere, wandering in and out of the rooms, shoving each other into the pool.

The Scotch coffee—the recipe was identical to that of Irish coffee, made instead with Drambuie—was a hit with Mr. Carstairs and his guests, but if I had hoped it would divert them from the promise of breakfast, I was mistaken. It was Texas Tamara, the show-girl, who started it. She was sitting on Mr. Carstairs' lap.

"Honey, you know what I would really love right now?" she said to him in her slow Southern drawl. "A bi-i-ig bowl of grits. With an egg in it." She turned to me expectantly. "That wouldn't be any trouble now, would it?"

Grits? What on earth were those? The name alone made my teeth feel as though I had a mouthful of sand. "I'm sorry, sir," I said, addressing my employer, "I've never had the opportunity to cook ... grits. I'm afraid I don't know what they are."

"Oh, we have them," he said, winning from her a hug and a kiss on the cheek. "They're in the pantry—they come in a box."

Tamara jumped off his knee and padded into the kitchen behind me. "I'll cook 'em, honey," she smiled at me. "You just watch, for next time."

I did watch, as did half of the other European guests who were equally at sea with regard to the mysterious food. She cooked up an enormous saucepan of what appeared to me to be thin wallpaper paste, dipped off a bowlful for herself, then with a flourish, added to her portion a large raw egg. The Europeans, who tried the leftovers, grimaced and pronounced it extremely fine, soggy porridge.

But the act of cooking had made the remainder of the party ravenous, and they clamored for food. For the next two hours I was a short-order cook, making up omelettes, fried bread, bacon butties, sausage-and-Branston-pickle sandwiches, and eggs of every description.

## Fifteen Hints for Averting Entertaining Emergencies

- Never serve just one dish, especially when it's something exotic—for example, seafood gumbo—without enough other side dishes to cover. If a guest is allergic to or dislikes a key ingredient in your dinner—shellfish—you will have no backup.
- Whatever the main course, serve lots of different vegetables—three or four varieties. Not only do vegetables add necessary color, but if you get an unexpected extra guest, you can reduce the size of entrée and still fill the plate.
- Many vegetables can be prepped in advance of use. The day you buy cauliflower, broccoli, carrots, green beans, and other "hard" vegetables, wash, pare, and cut them into bite-sized pieces. Then cover them with water in airtight containers, and refrigerate for up to a week. Fresh vegetables will always be available, regardless of how last-minute the meal may be.
- For impromptu barbecues, chicken thighs and drumsticks can be defrosted very quickly. Also, hamburger meat can be made into patties and frozen. Separate these with wax paper and wrap in freezer paper, not foil—the latter has a tendency to stick when you're in a hurry.
- A supply of ice cream, topped with frozen berries quickly thawed in the microwave, will always yield an easy, pretty dessert. Also, don't overlook your liquor cabinet. Liqueurs such as Kahlúa, crème de cassis, crème de menthe, Grand Marnier, Amaretto, Frangelica, or any cream liqueur such as Bailey's Irish Cream make elegant toppings for ice cream. Serving ice cream in footed glass bowls or large wine glasses with a single mint sprig adds extra flourish.
- A dish containing avocados is never a good choice for last-minute entertaining (unless they're in season and

*(continued on next page)*

*(continued from previous page)*

you have a tree in your garden). Avocados are ripe when they're soft, and for general recipe use should be purchased at least a week in advance.

- Make and freeze homemade soups, particularly when seasonal vegetables are most abundant. Heated and served with hot rolls or a loaf of fresh bread, it is one of the coziest meals possible on short notice.
- If you boil a chicken, reduce the liquid and freeze it. Chicken stock is the best base for soups, and homemade is still far superior to canned.
- Your freezer should always have frozen peas and corn. They are quick to cook and are great for adding color to any dish.
- Have at least four types of pasta on hand in the pantry. Most cook in less than fifteen minutes. The addition of sautéed fresh vegetables, some cream, and parmesan cheese results in pasta primavera, an excellent vegetarian alternative to omelettes.
- Frozen shrimp (30–40 count) and scallops, often available in 1½-pound bags in discount food warehouses, are invaluable. They can be defrosted in minutes and added to pasta, sautéed with garlic, butter, and wine and served with rice, or boiled briefly and served on ice with cocktail sauce—a perennially popular hors d'oeuvres.
- For picture-perfect vegetables, even when the meal is delayed, parboil the vegetables until *just* tender, then plunge them immediately into ice and cold running water. (This arrests the cooking process and also fixes the color.) After a few minutes in the cold bath, drain the vegetables and set aside. A few minutes prior to serving, finish cooking them by dropping them back into hot water, or by quickly sautéing them in butter for a couple of minutes. (Carrots finished this way are glistening.)

*(continued on next page)*

*(continued from previous page)*

- Try to prepare as much of a meal as possible in advance. If it is ready to go, you can delay or move a meal up if necessary. Choose recipes that can be made in advance, and simply finished off at the last minute. Pre-prepare salads, pâtés, soup. Even soufflés can be prepared to the stage of needing only the addition of the whipped egg whites.
- Buy food in season, in good supply. Never buy cheap provisions; quality will always win out. (I made the mistake of buying frozen fruit cocktail in bulk once. It was limp, tasteless, and without color, and no one finished it.)

I got to bed at 6 A.M., but was up by ten o'clock to get to the shops and replace the stores of Michel's larder. There were sleeping bodies on every sofa and armchair. People snored on the floor, in the hallway, under the dining room table, even outside by the pool. I daresay Mr. Carstairs had enjoyed himself. He didn't get up until two in the afternoon.

Enjoying himself, and ensuring that others did too, was Mr. Carstairs' goal. Particularly when he had visitors from the States, it was one whirlwind, nonstop party. I wouldn't say they drank a lot, but one gentleman named Mr. Novak, who came over, lost a whole day of his holiday. Mr. Carstairs met him at the Nice airport with a bottle of champagne, which they consumed in a limousine on the way back to the Monte Carlo flat. That night they went to a show, then round the clubs, then finally to breakfast, before they rolled in to Roquebrune at about 6 A.M. Mr. Novak went to bed and didn't wake up until 7 A.M.—more than twenty-four hours later.

Among Mr. Carstairs' visitors over the summer were his two daughters, Cindy and Debbie. In their late teens, tall and leggy with streaked blonde hair and a smattering of freckles over their noses, they certainly corresponded to my expectations of what California girls looked like. But their confusion was easy to see. In spite of the sun-seeking, general hilarity of life at the Maison du Gouverneur, their holiday was overshadowed by the news of their parents' impending divorce. Their world had been thrown into an uproar, and it was clear that they were struggling to adapt. Mr. Carstairs' carefree party atmosphere was at once fun and disquieting, and my presence added another unfamiliar note. Although they were cordial, the look of disbelief on Debbie's face as I served her dinner the first night she was there said clearly, "My dad's got a butler! I don't even believe this." It was clear that a lifestyle that included live-in domestic staff was, to Cindy and Debbie, beyond the pale.

Though I had lived and worked around Monte Carlo for nearly five years, the aspects of it I saw with Mr. Carstairs were so completely different from those of Mr. and Mrs. Bristol's world that I might have been in a different country.

First of all, there was the car. Driving a Ferrari 308 was a far different experience than the exceedingly luxurious, but far more staid Rolls Royce. I never drove him anywhere, in the sense of being a chauffeur. The car seated only two, and if I needed it for the day, I dropped him off at the flat in Monte Carlo. Or rather, he would drive, and I would take the car after we had arrived. Like everything else he did, he took it to the limit, driving fast, downshifting for greater engine performance, roaring round blind bends on the wrong side of the road just to scare his passengers (it worked). He loved fast cars, and once confided that he wished he could have raced professionally. But even when I drove it (at far more sedate speeds), it was impossible not to experience a feeling of *joie de vivre.*

Then there was the fact that he had me accompany him to extraordinary places. Once, because his friend Jean, who worked at the casino, was connected somehow to the Monagasque royalty, Mr. Carstairs obtained tickets for twenty concert seats to see the band Dire Straits—right in front of Princess Stephanie. At his insistence, I helped make up the party that included Mr. Carstairs, Debbie, Cindy, and a dozen of their friends.

"How on earth did you arrange for tickets in front of Princess Stephanie?" I asked, astonished, as I passed him smuggled alcoholic drinks in orange juice containers.

"Easy. Jean said they have to have people they know in front of her," he said with a grin. "So in case someone takes a pot shot at her, they'll get us first. You are wearing your bulletproof vest, aren't you?"

# 9

# Coming to America

Even all of Mr. Carstairs' informality could not have prepared me for America or the position I would occupy there.

In September we closed up the Maison du Gouverneur, and I packed Mr. Carstairs' personal effects for his journey back to the States. He had given me a week to see my family and friends in England, and to settle my affairs there before meeting him at Heathrow to fly to Southern California.

In the Mini I made a leisurely farewell trip through France before crossing the Channel and making my way to London. Coming back to my childhood home—now my investment—felt strange, but my father was glad to see me and excited that I was going to America. For the next few days I went round to the bank and building society to arrange for direct debit of his household bills from my bank account, and for someone from the Home Help Association to come in once a week and clean for him. I repaired a leaky tap in the kitchen of the house, and found storage for my Mini. I also looked up some of my old mates, most of whom I found during the evening in the same pub they had patronized when I had lived there. On the whole they were amused by what I did now.

"So you're some sort of Jeeves now, eh?" they ribbed me. "And you're off to America? Why? Maybe you could get a job at bloody Buckingham Palace!"

It wasn't long, though, before I began to notice a disquieting fact—my friends were virtually in the same place they had been when I had left for France seven years ago. They had their wives and children and their livings, but none of them seemed to see what they did as their career; rather, it was a job, a means of scraping by and paying for a few pints "down the pub" each night. More than half of the people I enquired after were on the dole, living in council flats subsidized by the government. The talk all round me was how so-and-so was "on the fiddle," or how so-and-so had a good trade as a roofer or mason, but worked strictly on a cash-only basis so as to avoid paying the value-added tax of over seventeen percent. Nowhere did I see the burning desire to succeed, to get ahead, to be somewhere else other than where they had been born. They were interested, but a little contemptuous of my stories of life in Paris, Cannes, Roquebrune, and on the boats. I could read on their faces their noncomprehension of why anyone would want to take up life outside what was known and comfortable. Complacency, combined with hopelessness, was thinly disguised as bravado.

After three days, I realized I didn't fit into the English way of life anymore. It was home, but to me it had stood still. It was my past, but in the United States, I felt, was my future. So, with only my two suitcases, I left England for the great unknown of America.

Mr. Carstairs had arranged a short-term working visitor's visa for me while he and an immigration lawyer set about getting me a "green card," the slang term for resident alien credentials. For legal reasons, throughout the term of my visa, I would continue to be paid through Mr. C's bank in Monte Carlo. In theory, I was coming to America to train a staff to run Mr. C's estate the way I had run his Monte Carlo house, to which I would afterwards return. In fact, although they did advertise the job statewide, they found that, of the only four applicants who answered the advertisement, none was qualified for the position. Two were illegal immigrants, one was married with four children, and the fourth could neither cook nor speak French. This cleared the way for the lawyer to apply for my permanent resident status on the basis that I was not taking a job away from an American. Even so, I was nervous that immigration at the Los Angeles airport was going to turn me away.

Someone from his company met us in a relatively small Cadillac limousine that I later learned I would use to chauffeur him.

"You'll want to pay attention to how we get home," he told me. "I'll need you to pick people up here pretty regularly. In fact, next week, I'm expecting someone, so you'll be coming back here then." Somewhat bleary-eyed, I tried to concentrate on the freeways, noting absently the sheer volume of cars on the four-lane roadway. And the license plates! Not only were there plates from all these other places I'd heard of—Arizona, Texas, Nevada, Oregon—I had never seen personalized license plates before.

Like London, Los Angeles seemed to be densely populated; but, unlike it, the sprawling metropolis didn't seem to ease once we had traveled twenty minutes away from the airport. Although the highway signs indicated that we were changing towns, there seemed to be no distinguishing features—simply one long, unbroken stretch of humanity.

Finally we turned off the freeway and began to wind through a surprisingly rural valley bordered by rolling, dry brown hills accented with stunted, glossy-leafed scrub oak trees. Then rather suddenly the canyon ended and before us stretched a wide golden beach, where the Pacific Ocean glimmered in the sunlight and a group of teenage boys played a manic game of basketball on the tarmac nearby.

Winding alongside the coast, we turned into a road blocked by enormous black gates with a small booth in which sat a uniformed guard. Mr. Carstairs nodded to the guard as the gates swung open, allowing us through. I sat up, alert once more. This must be it!

But to my surprise, behind the gates were many residences, not just one. We cruised slowly through an entire neighborhood of houses set incredibly close together, eventually pulling into a shallow semicircular driveway fronting a low, wooden ranch-style house. Wide brick steps led to a heavy oak front door. I had been told that everything in America was big, but even so, these were pretty impressive staff quarters.

"This will be very nice, sir," I said. "Where do you live?"

Mr. Carstairs' eyebrows shot up, then he began to laugh. "I live here. This is my house, Promontory Point."

Here? In this small house? After a fifty-four room *villa*! Oh God, I thought, as my heart sank into my stomach, I've made a dreadful mistake in coming here. This isn't a promotion for me.

He took me through the house, which, despite its looks, was far more roomy on the inside than it appeared. It was, he told me, forty-five hundred square feet. Still, there were only three bedrooms and a small guest wing, which, it seemed, I would occupy.

Inside as well as out there was a proliferation of wood—wooden-paneled walls, cathedral ceilings, parquet floors. An impressive stone fireplace dominated the sitting room off the front hall. The entire rear wall of the spacious room was comprised of glass that looked out past a sparkling turquoise pool over steep cliffs to the Pacific Ocean beyond. This same view was shared by the kitchen, dining room, family room, and all three spacious bedrooms, including the enormous master suite, which also featured a fireplace at the foot of the bed. A cozy private study, paneled in teak and fitted out like a captain's cabin aboard a ship, also contained its own fireplace. Under the house, the three-car garage contained a late model Buick Riviera, an old Pontiac convertible that would be my car, and a golf cart. His Ferrari, I knew, was being shipped out and would arrive in a few months. The house was part of a private community with its own beach down the road, which, I learned, was the purpose of the golf cart.

We went through the sliding French doors in the sitting

room to the patio. A Jacuzzi was set in the wooden deck, its side forming a waterfall into the large pool below. To one side, a pergola offered shaded seating, while a small strip of lawn bordered the space. A low, hedge-covered fence separated the property from the steep cliffs beyond. To the other side of the pool area was another rolling lawn, thick and deep blue-green.

"Where are the grounds?" I asked, as I continued to walk round the house. Spying a park-like quarter-acre of lawn adjoining the enclosed garden near my room, I pointed. "Is that yours as well?"

My consternation had apparently amused my employer. "No, no, you don't understand California real estate." At my puzzled look, he elaborated. "The Maison du Gouverneur, it was for sale, right? Do you know what they wanted for it?"

I nodded. I had checked. The asking price was the equivalent of close to two million U.S. dollars.

"Well, this house—and more to the point, the land it sits on—was recently appraised at nearly eight million dollars."

*This* place? I looked around, wide-eyed. I could see I had a lot to learn about America.

The large, airy room that was to be mine had vaulted ceilings, a walk-in wardrobe, and its own private entrance onto a beautifully landscaped front patio, from which one could also access the family room. Surrounding the patio was a rose garden and a small but lush green lawn rolled down to a bank of protective evergreens that shielded the garden from the street.

My uniforms and the small amount of casual clothing took up only a few feet in the large closet. I had come to America with little more than what I had carried with me over the past eight years: my uniforms and shoes, a dozen books, and a good-sized collection of homemade cassette tapes. My meager possessions rendered the room about as personal as I had found the Villa Bianco to be, years before.

I experienced my first taste of the variety of choice to be found in America the next day. Following Mr. C's directions

("The town? Turn right at the gate. You'll find everything."), I found my way into the beachside village and parked, walking through the busy streets to familiarize myself with the location of the shops, banks, petrol stations, and other things I was likely to need fairly quickly. Spotting a grocery store, I went in, as Mr. C had asked if I would pick up some milk. Although I was impressed by the enormity of the interior, when I found my way to the dairy section, I stopped in astonishment.

In contrast to England's familiar glass pint bottles, there stretched before me an endless array of milks, the like of which I'd never seen. Not only were there types called homogenized, half-and-half (of what?), heavy cream, low-fat, non-fat, and acidophilus (what on earth was *that*?) all in different colors, there were different brands and four different sizes of each. I strained my memory to remember if Mr. C had mentioned specifically what kind of milk he required, but drew a blank. After ten minutes of carefully reading each carton, I gave up and selected one at random and carried it to the checkout.

I selected wrongly, as it turned out. "No, no, I need the non-fat, the blue one," Mr. Carstairs said when he came home. But he was good natured about my mistake, laughing at my awe of American dairy sections.

My position at Promontory Point was that of a *majordomo*—the title for the position of multiple responsibility I had envisaged when working for Lady Welsh. As I had done in France, I shopped for and cooked Mr. C's meals and served them, and acted as chauffeur on the occasional circumstances when he required it, but that was just the beginning. I also kept the cars clean and running well, oversaw the thrice-weekly gardening service and twice weekly pool maintenance crews, ran all the errands, and fixed—or had fixed, if I couldn't do it myself—all the things that require occasional repair in the running of a household. One big difference was that, unlike in Europe, at Promontory Point I had no daily housekeeper. While a delightful, capable woman named

Sheilah came in once a week to clean the house and change the bed linen, I did the washing-up after meals, the laundry and ironing of both the household linen and his clothing, as well as keeping the house tidy in between her visits. Outside, I cleaned the garden furniture, kept the patio swept and hosed down, and the barbecue clean and at the ready. It was certainly a far cry from serving afternoon tea to Lady Welsh. At least I didn't do windows.

Another big difference was the dress requirements. When Mr. Carstairs came back to the house one morning to find me washing the cars in a shirt and tie, my usual day clothes, a comical look appeared on his face.

"Aren't you a little overdressed for that?" he said, amused.

"Sir?"

"I know I can be a hard-ass, but I don't go so far as to require a tie for car-washing duty. Save your ties for dinner, hmmm? In the meantime, go get yourself some jeans and T-shirts for daytime work." After years of black-and-whites, the idea of being able to wear jeans during the day was like being on holiday.

He was too informal a man to require daily valet service; my running him a bath and selecting and laying out his daily business suits would have been met with incredulity. My valet duties included taking care of his clothing and making sure everything was laid out in readiness for him for dress affairs, and packing for him when he went away. As my main responsibility was the upkeep and maintenance of his house, I did not travel with him. Instead, having made the acquaintance of his tailor, I shopped for him, packed for him, made all the travel arrangements, and dealt with his affairs in his absence, including many financial matters. He did travel a fair amount, both for business and pleasure. Having purchased the flat in Monte Carlo, he returned to the South of France for a few months at a time each year, as well as taking skiing holidays in the winter and trips to Hawaii and other tropical locales in the fall.

Another contrast to my far more formal position with Mr. and Mrs. Bristol was that I had a lot of interaction with Mr.

Carstairs' family. He had precipitated his divorce at a time when Debbie and Cindy were away at university, which meant that while they visited for periods of time they were not a part of the daily household. However, we saw a lot of Mr. C's girlfriend, Donna, and her two children by a previous marriage. In her late thirties, Donna was a striking half-Asian woman, the product, she told me, of a Polynesian mother and an American serviceman who had been stationed in the South Pacific during the war. Small boned and petite, she had hazel green, slightly almond-shaped eyes, a small straight nose with a smattering of freckles, long dark hair that she kept rinsed with red highlights, and wonderful legs. Although my job, theoretically, was to take care of Mr. C and his house, the reality was that he had strong ties to both his family and Donna's, and in his eyes, I was a resource to be used by all. The tasks I was asked to handle encompassed processing the necessary applications for foreign visas so that Debbie could study abroad, and packing up Cindy's possessions and arranging for shipment to her new apartment in another state. On a more everyday basis, I would often pick up Donna's kids and bring them back to the house for Sunday dinner, or take her car to be serviced, or go mend the hot water heater at her house.

I quickly learned that the most important requirement of my job was resourcefulness. Whether it was finding a book conservator to get a wine stain off a treasured letter from the President, a supplier for an obsolete drawer-pull, or a tree service to prune the evergreens that bordered the property, the challenge was to Find It, or Find Someone Who Can Find It.

Our association was not without some growing pains on both sides. If I was unprepared for the casual familiarity of Americans, Mr. C was equally surprised at some of my English customs. I hadn't been in California very long when he discovered that our choice of lunchtime beverages differed.

It was a beautiful day, and Mr. C, unbeknownst to me, had decided to come back from the office for an afternoon

### A Valet's Tips to Impeccable Clothing

- If you don't have a lint roller, a roll of scotch or masking tape, rolled inside out over your hand, will do in an emergency.
- Spots of coffee respond to cold water applied freely.
- Clothes aired out at the end of the day will require less dry cleaning, and last longer.
- Before washing anything, button buttons and zip zippers. Clothes will require less repair—that is, lost buttons—and retain their shape better.
- Iron trousers inside out, except when doing the crease. Use a damp tea towel between iron and the trouser leg to steam in the crease.
- Iron a shirt in the following order: sleeves and cuffs, yoke, back, collar, and, finally, front. In this way there is less chance of the front (the most visible) being recreased after ironing. Hang, fastening *at least* the top button and third button down, or fold immediately for drawers or shelves.
- Hang suit jackets on padded or wooden hangers over a sheet of acid-free tissue paper draped round the hanger neck. Scrunch tissue paper and enclose it in another sheet of tissue paper to form a tube, then insert the tubes into the sleeves.
- Wear plastic gloves when shining shoes. Someone always seems to come to the door when your hands are streaked with polish.
- Melted Kiwi shoe wax applied to leather shoes with the back of a hot spoon (wear gloves!) helps to reduce the creases in the tops of the shoes. Always finish by buffing with a very, very soft cloth.
- When polishing buttons, buckles, or metal ornaments on clothing or shoes, cut a slit in a small piece of cardboard from a cereal box. Slipping the cardboard under the button will protect the coat against cleaning fluid stains.

*(continued on next page)*

*(continued from previous page)*

- An easy way to do emergency darning on socks is to stuff an orange inside the toe.
- For traveling, pack trousers in a suitcase that is wide enough so they only have to be folded once. Stuff tissue paper into the folds to prevent creases.
- To prevent garments from wrinkling when traveling, place them in individual plastic dry-cleaning bags. Fold each garment into the suitcase in overlapping layers—for example, the bottom half of a jacket, followed by top half of a skirt, bottom half of a blouse, the bottom of the skirt, the top of the blouse, the top of the jacket—so that each piece of clothing is cushioned by another.
- Shoes should be packed in plastic or fabric shoe bags and packed along the hinge of the suitcase, together with other heavy articles. Roll undergarments and socks and stuff into corners and edges of suitcase.
- For long-term storage of clothes, pack garments in tissue paper in sturdy boxes. Inventory the contents and make three copies of the list: one should be placed inside the box, one should be taped to the outside of the box, and one should be stored in a manila file.

swim. I had just made myself a sandwich for lunch, and was carrying it with my beer to the patio, when the back door opened and Mr. C came in. As he saw me, a look of consternation creased his brow.

"Good God! What are you doing?"

I looked around, surprised. "Having lunch, sir. Is there something wrong?"

Comprehension dawned on his face. "D'ya know, Chris," he said wryly, "if you were in my office, I'd fire you right now?"

"Why?"

"Because you're having a drink at lunchtime."

"Oh, no, sir. I'm having a beer."

"But a beer is considered a drink here. And drinking at lunchtime is against my company rules. It's against the rules of most American companies."

I raised an eyebrow. In England we drink beer the way Americans drink water. "I see, sir."

"So this time, we'll just consider it part of our joint learning experience, okay? But in the future, please wait until you're off duty before you pop a cold one, hmmm?"

This direct approach I found to be typical of Mr. Carstairs' management style, for in spite of the variety, working for him was very straightforward. On the first day, he had handed me a notebook and requested that I please take notes while he gave me a quick rundown of Promontory Point and its routine. In old-money houses that were accustomed to having domestic staff, this sort of business-like approach to staff management would have been unheard of; servants were expected to basically mind-read. But Mr. C had been in the military, and subscribed to the orderliness and infallibility of written lists, a habit I have since found invaluable.

Highly disciplined himself, he preferred the structure of his home life to be consistent, with few deviations and no surprises. To that end, he would specify—once—what he wanted, how he wanted it done, and make sure I had the resources necessary, then expect thereafter I should handle the same situation in an identical manner. This is not to say that he was staid or boring; rather, it simply meant that a certain request or statement that he was going to do something translated into a series of actions on my part to ensure that his experience would be smooth and predictable. For example, a highly stressful day at the office would elicit from him a phone call to me as he was leaving: "I need to take a swim." I would therefore know that he'd had a hard day and to wipe down the golf cart, make sure the battery it ran on was fully charged, and park it outside, ready to go. On the cart would be a small radio, a thick towel, and a cooler containing a carton of milk and a few bottles of grapefruit juice and beer, all on ice. His swimming trunks would be laid out on his bed. Upon his arrival, he'd change without a word and take the golf cart to the beach for a half-hour swim to work off his frustration.

Although he could be demanding, this preference for routine was actually one of the nicest things about working for him. One knew exactly where one stood with him. After the first request, I would know precisely what he wanted in a given situation, and if I then failed in the endeavor, he would be disappointed in me. Conversely, however, there were no hidden agendas or land mines; nothing came out of the woodwork. If, for example, he asked for coffee, I wouldn't find out, upon bringing it, that he'd actually wanted a coffee drink made with Drambuie and whipped cream. Or, on the rare occasions that he had wanted something extra, he was apologetic. "Sorry; forgot to tell you," he'd say. He never, ever got angry at me. This rational, logical approach to management both taught me a lot, and did a lot for me, as it gave me control over my job that was unheard of in previous years.

Cooking was a big part of my job at Promontory Point. I cooked and served meals five nights per week—of which at least three were dinner parties—and did a weekly barbecue of hamburgers, chicken, and fish for the children and whoever else was around each Sunday. On Tuesday evenings, when I was off, I left him a cold meal.

"I'm over the limit on my weight again, you have to get me down," he'd tell me once in a while. This would mean that I was to put him on a diet that cut out all fat, which translated into lots of salads, vegetables, and grilled fish with lemon and chives. And although he entertained a lot, no one else "suffered" his diets. I might do poached fish or chicken with a sauce that, for him, was on the side.

Mr. C's discipline and high personal expectations were often felt by those close to him as well. I had seen him more than once—in the presence of other guests at a dinner party—gesture tipsily towards Donna and announce, "You get fat, my girl, and you're outta here."

Although she responded under these circumstances with a

laughing, "Oh, shut up, Jack," I was aware she worried (unnecessarily, in my opinion) about gaining weight. I knew when cooking for her to unobtrusively put her sauces on the side, dress her salads with only lemon juice, and give her the smallest possible portions of each course without attracting attention by doing so.

The hours were long, even by domestic service standards. It was typical for me to work eighty hours a week when he was in town, forty when he was away. Unlike working for Lady Welsh, there was almost no "down time," such as that spent waiting for her in the car. Each day I had my list of errands and chores, as well as the meals to do. I had one full day off, on Friday, in addition to Tuesday night when I played darts (I had joined a league in order to meet people), and I wasn't due on duty until noon on Sunday morning, theoretically so I could attend church services.

Mr. Carstairs justified to himself the long hours I put in as being offset when he traveled; he thought that in his absence, I would spend all my time at the beach. This was patently ridiculous, as he would leave me enormous "to do" lists that included huge projects such as cleaning and oiling the teak-paneled study, stripping and resealing the wooden decks, and treating the exterior of the wooden shingle house. The first time he went away, I put in almost as many hours as I did when he was home in order to get it all done, and it taught me a lesson. The next time, I stood up for myself.

"I'm sorry, sir, but there is too much here to be done in the time allowed," I said. "What are the priorities as far as you're concerned?"

I think he was taken aback, but he rattled off four or five of the items. "Get those done, and anything else will be gravy," he said.

I still never made it to the beach, but at least I maintained "normal" working hours and was allowed to cultivate a life for myself.

My pay the first year was negligible, but because I had been promised a green card granting me legal residency, which Mr. C assured me was costing him hefty lawyer's fees,

I didn't approach him for a pay rise. This process of legalization was another reason that once I came to America, I didn't travel with him again—it wasn't worth the risk of deportation. But, unlike Lady Welsh, in Mr. Carstairs' absence I was allowed to have guests of my own in the house. The first year I was with him, since I was unable to go back to England, I brought my father to California to visit for several weeks. His enjoyment of the trip made it an annual event thereafter.

During my second year, he entrusted me with the responsibility of overseeing the renovation of one wing of Promontory Point while he was away. He had, with me present, approved the plans of contractors and designers, but I was to ensure that it came out the way he wanted it—and on budget. Therefore, I would be given sole signing authority over a hundred thousand dollar account, with the simple request to make sure the project was a success. The fact that it did succeed launched me into a new phase of estate management, one that has since served me well. In successive years with him I negotiated and oversaw the redesigning of the guest suites (formerly those of Debbie and Cindy), the kitchen, and, finally, my quarters.

The kitchen was my most hands-on project, as I used it daily and knew its strengths and weaknesses. When I proposed, after the wing renovation, that his next major project be a full kitchen remodel, he was open to the suggestion but issued a challenge—research and price it, he said, then come back with a proposal and he would look at it.

This sort of free reign was stimulating to me, as I relished the opportunity to expand my knowledge base. After working with architects, designers, and contractors, as well as spending considerable time evaluating equipment and options, I laid my finished proposal before him.

"Why did you choose that stove?" he questioned.

"Because, sir, it has these features"—I noted them—"but it doesn't have these"—I listed some trendy options that were enjoying great popularity, then explained why he didn't need them. I knew immediately that I'd scored a hit with this approach. He loved being told what he didn't need, and why.

"What about the wine cellar? Can we build it in under the stairs?" In true military form, he hated wasted space with no function. I had anticipated this idea.

"I looked at that option, sir, and it can be done, but . . . " I presented the quotes I had received, all of which were for about six thousand dollars. "Whereas, for $1,400, you can buy a stand-alone wine cellar. I have it built in here"—I indicated an area in the butler's pantry.

After grilling me at length about each item I presented, he finally stood up.

"You've done well, Chris," he said. "You know the value of a dollar. That'll get you far."

I did the kitchen remodel the following autumn.

Something else that tended to happen when Mr. Carstairs went away was that he would mention to his family and to his neighbor, Mr. Vanders, that I might be available if they needed me. In the case of Mr. Vanders, who couldn't seem to keep good staff, it was a pleasure, as a chauffeuring job or a dinner party would mean substantial extra money to me.

Mr. Vanders, who was a divorced man as well, liked to entertain a great deal. His large house, Villa Ventana, was only two years old and built to resemble the white stucco estates found in Greece and southern Italy. Periodically he would hire me to do a dinner party, always paying me a generous wage, and often a nice tip as well. But the nicest tip he ever gave me wasn't in cash. His daughter was getting married, and Mr. Vanders, who owned some beautiful vintage automobiles, had asked if he could hire me for the day to act as their chauffeur, driving his candy-apple red, fully restored 1938 Packard Super 8 convertible.

Would I? I jumped at the opportunity, paid or unpaid, to drive this incredible car. It had a long, long bonnet,with a gleaming radiator grill that came to a point like a ship's prow, topped with an impressive winged hood ornament. Large, curving front fenders that swept down and away past side-mounted spare tires acted as eyebrows over the spotless whitewall tires. The well-serviced engine turned over immediately and purred, lionlike. It was an honor to be trusted to sit in the vehicle, much less drive it. I purchased a chauffeur's cap for the occasion, and spent an effortless sixteen-hour day motoring my charges from home to church to reception to hotel. I'm not sure who had more fun, the bridal couple or me.

"I owe you one," a grateful Mr. Vanders told me at the end of the night, as he paid me for my time. "Someday I'll repay the favor." The favor? As far as I was concerned, the debt was mine, just for having been able to drive such a splendid automobile.

Yet three years later, when I got engaged, Mr. Vanders was as good as his word. In addition to his congratulations, he offered the Packard as transportation from our reception.

Amidst appreciative calls of our friends and family, Kim and I waved from the rear seat as the shimmering red convertible pulled away from the Tudor-style restaurant in which our wedding celebration had been held. In the driver's seat, Mr. Vanders tipped his chauffeur's cap with a grin.

I believe I must be the only butler in existence to have had a billionaire chauffeur drive him from his wedding reception!

# 10

# A Butler's-eye View of American Holidays

"Thanksgiving is next Thursday," Mr. Carstairs said one morning in mid-November. "Donna, the kids, and her parents are coming for dinner. Just so you know, you'll need to pick them up at the airport on Wednesday afternoon. For the most part, let's just have a traditional meal. Donna'll help with the food and all."

Donna was to help me? With only six guests? "Fine, sir. Um, sir . . . what, exactly, is the traditional meal?"

He looked at me for a moment, unsure whether or not I was being funny, then grinned lopsidedly. "Oh yeah—Thanksgiving isn't a holiday in England, is it? Roast turkey with stuffing, candied yams, mashed potatoes, creamed vegetables, and pumpkin pie are considered traditional here. Donna can give you more details. Talk to her."

Pumpkin *pie*? What strange things Americans ate.

Throughout the next six weeks life was hectic indeed. At Mr. C's request I purchased and decorated the Christmas tree, and strung exterior lights around the outside of the house and in the enormous pine tree at the front of Promontory Point. He made gift lists and had me shop for Donna and her kids and Debbie and Cindy, as well as other friends and acquaintances. He also put me in charge of coordinating the ordering of Christmas gifts for his ninety employees, each of whom were given the choice, in advance, of a large turkey, ham, or beef roast.

In addition, between Thanksgiving and Christmas, Mr. Carstairs entertained six to eight guests every night. I found something almost manic in his schedule, until I remembered it was the first Christmas since his divorce. He had, apparently, always thanked friends and business associates before Christmas by having them to dinner; he was simply trying to maintain "business as usual."

After the whirlwind buildup to Christmas, the day itself seemed almost to be a letdown for him. Debbie and Cindy had chosen to spend the holiday with their mother, and he had celebrated the previous evening with Donna and her two children. His younger brother and family and old Mr. Carstairs senior came for Christmas Day. In the kitchen, I answered phone call after phone call from friends and family ringing to wish him a happy Christmas. The meal was straightforward–he had asked for another turkey dinner "with all the fixings," as he called it, and his father brought homemade apple pies. They spent most of the time in the Jacuzzi and in front of the television, so it was a fairly quiet day —until late in the afternoon, when an odd smell began to infiltrate the house.

As I brought in a pitcher of laced eggnog, Mr. C motioned to me. "God, Chris, do you smell it?"

I'd been in the kitchen doing the washing-up and hadn't noticed, but there in the living room there *was* an unfamiliar, distinctly unpleasant odor; pungent and almost sickly sweet. I walked around the rooms, trying to localize the smell. It seemed to be strongest in his bedroom–horrors–and in the living room, near the deck. It stuck to my skin and clothes, almost as though I had walked through a spray mister. I'd never smelled anything like it before, and said so.

"Oh, I know what it is all right–it's a skunk," he said. "It must be trapped somewhere under the house. You've got to get rid of it, fast, before New Years, or we're in deep shit.

## A Decorative Napkin Fold

For a truly formal dinner, your napkins should be white damask, folded simply (if monogrammed, with the monogram facing the diner) and placed directly on the service plate. Only if the first course is already at the table when guests are seated is it correct to place the napkin to the side of the plate.

For less than "black tie," however, creative napkin folding can add dimension and flair to your table. One of my favorite napkin folds is called the Bird of Paradise, as the points of the napkin fan out like the flowers of the plant of the same name. It is designed to be placed in a goblet or wineglass, adding height to the table. For the design, use a large, starched square napkin, and if it is printed, make sure that it looks good on both sides.

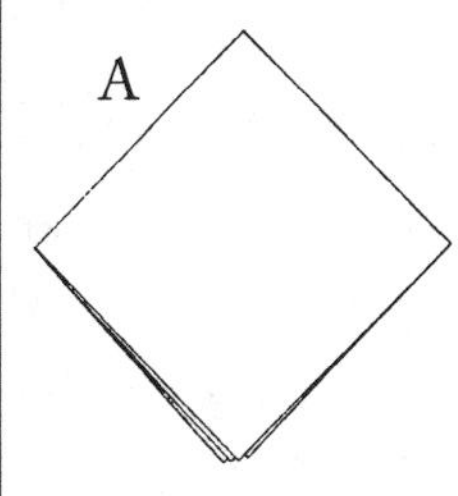


Fold a large, square napkin in half, then in half again to form a smaller square (A). All four corners should be together.

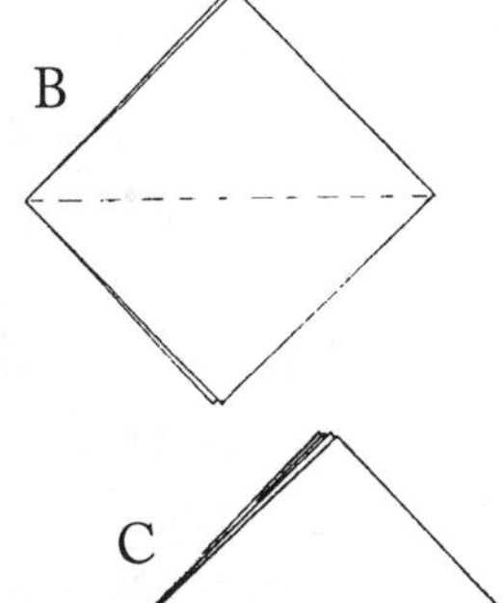


Take two of the corners and bring them to the opposite corner (B). Fold the remaining two corners backwards, to the same corner (C). You should now have a triangle.

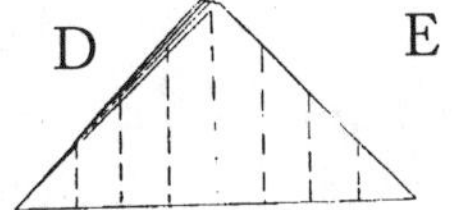

Beginning at one end, accordion-fold the triangular napkin (D).

Then, holding the base, carefully pull the outside-most material down on each side (E). Continue with the next layer, then pull the center out slightly.

Carefully set the finished napkin in your wineglass.

Not tonight, though," he added, as I started to head to the bedroom to change clothes. "Nah, just get us another drink. Hell, if we have enough, we'll be too bombed to smell anything!"

Although it was fifty degrees outside, I opened the doors and windows to get cross-ventilation, and sprayed lots of Mountain Floral air freshener throughout the house. Still, the pervasive aroma of skunk hung about.

The following morning I was down at the hardware store when it opened, where I bought wire mesh and other materials to flush out our unwanted tenant. Starting with the raised wooden pool deck, where a trap door allowed scant access to the plumbing and electrical equipment, I slunk round with a flashlight, looking for (though admittedly, not eager to find) beady eyes shining in the blackness. But there was no indication of a skunk's presence, and with some reluctance, I turned to the house.

There was no basement at Promontory Point; only a crawl space eighteen inches high, and most of the remainder of the day found me wriggling under the house on my belly. The cloying scent assured me I was looking in the right place. Knowing little about skunks other than they sprayed when they felt threatened, I could only assume our entertaining schedule had unnerved our lodger, for areas of highly concentrated scent were to be found on the concrete footings and the ductwork for the floor-mounted forced-air heating system. Finally, I found what looked to be a nest, near the base of the chimney, but no actual skunks; and when I had satisfied myself that it, or they, were out for the day, I affixed wire mesh to all the external openings I could find. Just to be safe, I also caulked from underneath all the loose-fitting grills on the central heating system, sprinkled liberal quantities of Skunk Away! on the ground, and backed my way out.

I presume the skunk or skunks sought new quarters upon finding themselves evicted, as they never bothered us again. No amount of Skunk Away!, however, could rid my clothing of all traces of our housemate, and after three washings I finally threw them away. However, each time the heater came on over the next week, a faint trace of Eau de Skunk rose from the floor grills to remind us of our Christmas visitors.

The New Years' Day party was one of two popular fetes that the Carstairs had thrown each year, and like the pre-Christmas dinner parties, my presence allowed Mr. C's divorced status to put no real cramp in his style of entertaining. Starting at midday and running until late evening, the New Years' party was an open house with a hot and cold buffet and, of course, lots of holiday cheer. Printed invitations had been sent out several weeks in advance, and now the RSVPs poured in by note and telephone until it appeared that we would have nearly one hundred guests attending.

Two days after Christmas, Debbie and Cindy arrived, as did another couple who were staying for the week, and the nightly dinner parties resumed. While Mr. C's eating habits were such that I rarely made him a meal other than dinner, his houseguests were not similarly inclined; the two girls in particular enjoyed the novelty of having breakfast made for them. In between times I worked feverishly to put the open house together, creating the menu, taking inventory of bar stocks, bar glasses, china, linen, and serving-ware. The whole of the last two days of December were spent polishing the silver, setting out the chafing dishes and arranging the flow of the buffet, and shopping for and prepping as much of the food as possible.

Mr. C was dining out on New Years' Eve—his first meal out since before Thanksgiving. He and Donna, Debbie and Cindy, and their dates, and his houseguests were all going to his country club for a gala dinner dance. The only trouble was that such an event required my services as a chauffeur, when I really needed a quiet evening to finish some of the last-minute preparations for the party. If I spent all night hanging about inside a limousine in a car park, I'd probably break out in hives.

The morning of the gala, as I washed and waxed the limousine and stocked the interior with champagne and booze, my head was abuzz with party details I needed to handle. At lunchtime, unable to stand it anymore, I spoke to Mr. Carstairs.

"Sir, are you likely to want to leave the gala before midnight?"

"What, early? Us? Not likely at all."

"Then if it's acceptable to you, after driving you to the club tonight, I'd like to come back here and work more on the party rather than waiting there. I'd be back by midnight, or whenever you specified, to pick you up."

"Fine by me," he said. He glanced round the kitchen where ample evidence of my preparations were evident and nodded thoughtfully. I believe he considered for the first time the amount of work his annual party entailed.

Even with all the advance preparation, the party itself was a long, long day. I had arranged for Sheilah to come in for six hours to help replenish the trays and chafing dishes, pass hors d'oeuvres and keep the buffet area and kitchen as tidy as possible, and her presence was a godsend to me. Equally present but less of a blessing were the girls and Donna, whose erratic help was not without some strain. There seemed to be a subtle power struggle going on between them as to who should assume the role of hostess. Mr. Carstairs remained purposefully oblivious to the tension, and I had no time to worry about them. On top of it all, other guests also brought food items, resulting in a general hubbub of "Where shall I put this?" and "Do you mind if I use your microwave to heat this up?" and a lot of people underfoot, mostly ineffectively.

The menu I had planned contained brunch, lunch, and appetizer selections. At his request there were a few items that appeared every year: platters of shrimp with cocktail sauce, a large glass bowl of fresh fruit salad, and Swedish meatballs made from his mother's recipe. Other components included chafing dishes full of lasagna, scrambled eggs, potatoes Lyonnaise, bacon, and sausage; hot baked ham and roast beef that I had carved and displayed next to baskets overflowing with miniature rolls with which to make bite-sized sandwiches; crudites and dips and crackers and chips. Frittatas, which I'd made in advance, were reheated in the oven and sent out like mini omelettes.

The large-screen televisions in the family room and master bedroom were tuned to the football games. Mr. Carstairs and most of the men were ensconced on sofas and chairs in front of them, cheering loudly, while most of the women chatted in groups in the living room and outside on the patios and decks. In between carving and refilling, I ran back and forth to the bar to restock the pitchers of heavily spiked Bloody Marys. I was replenishing the drink supply when I heard a sharp crack from the vicinity of the family room, where the buffet line was laid out. Excusing myself, I hurried to the table.

An extinguished can of Sterno lay on its side. On top and all around it lay the remains of a Pyrex dish that had contained a casserole of Italian sausage and peppers. Bits of the casserole dotted adjacent dishes, the wall, and the cream-colored carpet. Sheilah was already there, trying to clean up the chaos.

"Where did the bain-marie dish go?" I asked her in a low voice. It was evident that someone had taken away the chafing dish's proper pan and set the glass casserole dish directly over the Sterno fuel, and I knew it hadn't been Sheilah.

"God knows," she said. "There's a number of ladies here who keep trying to help. I thought I'd sorted them all out, but I certainly missed this."

As we mopped up the mess, Donna detached herself from a group on the patio and hurried over. "What happened?"

As I explained, a chagrined look came over her face. "Oh, I'm sorry, that was me," she said. "Marcia brought that, and I was just trying to heat it up a little faster." She looked so forlorn, I felt sorry for her. But thankfully, thereafter when she volunteered to help, she asked for directions, and confined her efforts as a hostess to attending to the guests.

There are a couple of inviolable rules one should observe when hiring domestic staff, particularly those who live in. The first, and most obvious, is to pay them fairly. As is said in the trade, the top three reasons staff leave for other positions are money, money, and money. Yet many employers assume that a position with room and board is worth enough that the actual cash remuneration can be negligible. "After all," they reason, "if I'm providing them with a place to live, food to eat, health insurance, and the use of a car, what do they really need except a little spending money?" What they fail to take into account is compensation necessary for the extremely long hours and lack of privacy.

The second inviolable rule is to treat the agreed-upon days off as though they are written in stone. It becomes very easy to forget that staff wish to have a life of their own outside that of their employers'. Because of the long hours in close proximity to his employer, a live-in domestic worker is doubly anxious for his time off in order to put together some semblance of a life of his own. When an employer pipes up with "Oh, George, d'ya mind working on Wednesday night and taking Thursday off instead? Wednesday is the only night the MacKenzies and the Collins are both free for dinner," it is very likely that George *does* mind, as he has arranged to meet friends for supper, have a horse-riding lesson, or engage in some other activity.

Mr. and Mrs. Whitfield, who lived down the street from Mr. Carstairs, were one of the few other occupants in the neighborhood to employ live-in domestic staff. Their sprawling Tudor-style house had actually been built with staff quarters, but these quarters saw a constant parade of occupants. The Whitfields—or more accurately, Mrs. Whitfield—seemed to have a problem keeping staff because she consistently violated these two caveats. Arrogant and capricious, she was prone to impulsive entertaining and expected her majordomo to juggle his days off to accommodate her. While once or twice such a change can be brought about with no ill will, in Mrs. Whitfield's case it happened repeatedly. On top of it all, she didn't pay enough to make such an affront acceptable.

This affected me with regularity, as Mr. C volunteered my services to help orient each of the housekeepers or majordomos Mrs. Whitfield hired. They ran the gamut from illegal immigrants who barely spoke English to highly trained professionals, but they all had one thing in common—they didn't last more than six months in the Whitfields' employ.

The first summer I was in California, they engaged a South American chap named Arturo, who was prone to name-dropping his previous employers and boasting of his broad expertise. I found him long on talk but short on initiative, and absolutely incompetent when it came to doing anything mechanical, like change a Hoover bag.

Once a year Mr. Carstairs and the Whitfields got together to throw their annual Fourth of July party, which I was expected to coordinate with whomever was currently on staff at the Whitfields'. The party itself was an odd mixture of casual and formal; a barbecue with a touch of silver service for seventy people. Until mid-afternoon the staff tended bar and passed hors d'oeuvres on silver trays; afterwards people would help themselves to heaping paper plates of food at the buffet table, while we manned the barbecue. Libations flowed freely from mid-morning until late in the evening. Guests wandered back and forth between the beach and both houses, playing tennis, softball, and football, and there was always an interesting small party that went on all afternoon in the swimming pool and Jacuzzi. Later, when it got dark, Mr. Carstairs and some of the other gentlemen lit off an impressive display of fireworks.

Each year the two houses would switch off, one providing the main course, the other the alcohol. This year the Whitfields were supplying the food. The menu itself was simple—various canapés to be passed, the Avocado Marie Rose as a starter, barbecued hotdogs and hamburgers, corn on the cob and baked beans, fresh fruit and various other cold salads, and large deep-dish pans of warm apple crisp with ice cream for dessert. This didn't, however, mean that Arturo alone was responsible for its preparation. The size of the party, and in my case, Mr. Carstairs' insistence on the freshest of ingredients meant a lot of pre-party preparation for us both, although I doubted I would be doing this party with him again the following year.

The day before the party, I met with Arturo in the Whitfields' kitchen to start prepping. All around the granite countertops were heads of lettuce, tomatoes, and onions for the hamburgers and green salads, as well as pineapples, melons, flats of strawberries, seedless grapes, and other fruits that would become fresh fruit salad. Condiments of every kind were stacked in the pantry.

I opened the Sub Zero refrigerator expecting to see packages of hamburger waiting to be seasoned and formed into patties. Instead I saw two large white cardboard boxes.

"Arturo? Did you already do the hamburgers?" Egads, I thought, perhaps he had more initiative than I had given him credit for.

"I do better than that." With a flourish he opened one of the cardboard boxes. Inside, separated by thin sheets of white waxy paper, dozens of thin, pale pink, machine-made rounds of hamburger, such as those found in fast food establishments, were reemerging from the ice age. Opening the meat compartment, he displayed boxes of industrial turkey franks, while the freezer was stuffed with plastic bags of frozen corn on the cob. "Mr. Whitfield, he send me to a food warehouse, tell me to buy these. They save on time, no?"

My heart sank as I looked at his provisions, knowing Mr. Carstairs would hate it. I wondered, not for the first time, how some people with lots of money can choose to buy second-rate materials in the belief they're saving a bob or two. Perhaps it's how they get rich in the first place.

Long-distance guests began to arrive the day before the party, filling all the spare beds and even the pull-out couch in Mr. C's family room. At 6 A.M. the day of the party, I tiptoed past sleeping forms and headed for the Whitfields' so that Arturo and I could get an early start setting up. Mr. Whitfield owned enough catering-quality tables and chairs to seat a hundred, so we hauled them from his basement and began to decorate the area. At 8 A.M. the ice was delivered, and we packed beers and sodas into large stainless steel tubs, then made batches of homemade ice cream and packed them into old-fashioned wooden buckets. We cut up gallons of fresh fruit for the salad, and assembled the last-minute food, such as the hors d'oeuvres, shrimp, and avocados.

People started to arrive around 1 P.M., but fortunately most headed straight down to the beach for a few hours, allowing us to prep relatively unimpeded. Around mid-afternoon, they started coming back in droves, and we began the hors d'oeuvres service. As Mr. C's back garden faced west, people would congregate there over drinks and hors d'oeuvres until sunset, then meander over to the Whitfields', where the barbecue was set up.

Mr. C had provided the decorations (which, incidentally, did my former employer, Mr. Griffith, proud): paper tablecloths, yards of bunting, and scads of small American flags with which we had created centerpieces for the buffet table and bar. On the dinner tables, card-shop accordion-fold paper centerpieces were augmented, at my request, with red and white carnations. American flags in profusion were stuck into planter containers, and dozens were stuck into a plastic Uncle Sam top hat on the bar, to be taken and waved. Everything—paper tablecloths, plates, and napkins—was printed in red, white, and blue with the American flag. Whether the effect was intentionally corny I didn't dare ask.

As Independence Day certainly wasn't *my* holiday, I had had (with Mr. Carstairs' permission) a barbecue apron made up that read: "Come back, Colonials—All is Forgiven!" which caused chuckles throughout the day.

I was still tending the busy bar somewhere around sunset when I sent Arturo back to set up the buffet in preparation for dinner. While I needed to get the barbecue started, because of Arturo's demonstrated lack of mechanical expertise, I didn't trust him to do it for me. Especially since the brand new Weber belonged to Mr. Whitfield, and was the biggest charcoal barbecue I'd ever seen.

I had been delayed restocking the beer tubs when Mr. Whitfield himself came up.

"Going great," he said in his usual jovial fashion. "Anything I can do?"

"Yes, sir," I said with some relief. Here was just the man to know the ins and outs of that enormous grill. "Could you light the barbecue for me?"

"Sure thing," he said, and wandered away with his beer.

But when I reached the barbecue station thirty minutes later, I found I had been seriously mistaken in my assessment.

Mr. Whitfield had obviously dumped the entire forty-pound bag of charcoal into the Weber, and probably with the help of a half-can of lighter fluid, got the charcoal started. The fire was so hot that without a pair of asbestos gloves, which we didn't have, I couldn't get near it.

Guests who had been working up an appetite all day gathered, watching hungrily while we waited for the barbecue to cool sufficiently to cook the meat. But an hour passed with no respite. The hamburgers, not thick in the first place, immediately became disks of carbon when I tried to put them on the grill.

Finally, in desperation I had Arturo stand guard over the fire while I dug through Mr. Whitfield's basement until I found his old barbecue. Running back to the party, I shoveled some of the charcoal into the old barbecue, and the fire abated to a point where it was usable.

Once dinner was well underway, I took a quick look around. But passing through the kitchen, I noticed, to my horror, the seven platters of Avocado Marie Rose forgotten on the counter. More than half of the guests had eaten by the time we put them out, with the result that nearly a third of the starters languished untouched in the tepid air and later had to be thrown away. I made sure to do so in the Whitfields' dustbin, knowing how much Mr. Carstairs hated to see anything go to waste. Fortunately for me, I thought, Mr. Carstairs was too happily intoxicated to notice the omission.

People started taking their leave around 9 P.M., which meant that Arturo's and my cleanup of both houses could then begin. Stomach rumbling—although the constant interaction with food had made eating unthinkable—I finally fell into bed around 12:30 A.M. I was disappointed that we hadn't had a chance to see the fireworks. Oh well, I thought, numb with exhaustion. It wasn't my holiday, after all.

The next morning, as I expected, Mr. C brought up the quality of the meat.

"Next year, I want to do it better. I want real handmade hamburgers, and no cafeteria-quality wieners. And good buns. And platters of shrimp and fresh vegetables. And fresh corn on the cob. And a choice of flavors for the homemade ice cream. And, Chris?"

"Sir?"

"Make sure the avocado things are on the table when the dinner starts, huh?"

# 11

# "Part of the Show"

Having an English butler was great fun for Mr. Carstairs; and as he entertained at home three and sometimes four nights per week, there was ample opportunity to show off his find. Generally he preferred relatively small parties of six to eight, which was, thankfully, the maximum for which I could cook and serve alone, without sacrificing quality and presentation.

Something that struck me as curious occurred at the first dinner party I did for him at Promontory Point, and continued at every one thereafter—Mr. Carstairs *introduced* me. I suppose it was inescapable that he do so, as my presence when I opened the door would occasion a slight start from his guests.

"Oh! A real live butler?" they would exclaim, all but circling me as though I were an exhibit in a museum, or worse, a zoo. But after a few weeks, I grew used to being a performer and began to play it to my advantage. They liked a show; why not give it to them? Among other things, I made sure that regardless of the informality of our everyday exchanges, I was always impeccably correct and formal with Mr. Carstairs in company. His parties were usually casually dressy to dressy affairs, but regardless of their formality I wore a tuxedo and black bowtie. It was part of the costume, part of the image.

Dinner was always called for eight o'clock, with guests arriving between seven and seven-thirty for cocktails. I greeted them at the door, took their wraps, and filled their drink orders. As they were small parties, there was little need for me to pass hors d'oeuvres; offering a tray once, then setting it down in a central location was sufficient and allowed me to get back to any final preparations for dinner I needed to make.

Dinner would be in varying states of preparation in the large corridor kitchen: vegetables prepped and ready in the steamer; meat marinaded or dressed, awaiting the final cooking; starters plated and in the refrigerator. White wine as an aperitif was open and on hand at the bar; red wine for dinner (and the occasional guest who preferred it to a cocktail) was breathing on the sideboard. Lights were turned low in the dining room. Candles would be lit at the last minute before I announced dinner. The polished mahogany table, capable of seating twelve, was set with the china most complementary to the meal I was serving—for example, the Spode china, with its masculine nautical pattern set off the roast veal in hunter sauce well. I found little things such as this made all the difference in the presentation of the meal.

For people unaccustomed to servants, I believe the idea of live-in household staff was harder on the women than it was the men, as they seemed to see me as a paid version of themselves. My position, particularly that aspect of it apparent at a dinner party, was a strange no-man's land between masculine and feminine, and often the female guests would wind up wandering into the kitchen to see how I was getting on. Shooing the ladies from the kitchen without being thought haughty or abrupt was a skill in itself.

"Those munchies—" (*munchies*?) "—you brought out, especially those little salmon things, were yummy, Christopher. How did you make them?"

"Oooh, what have you got simmering here?"

"Christopher, I was telling Marjorie about that marvelous

fillet of sole en croute you did for us last time we were here. Can I get the recipe? I want to do it for my women's group next month."

Mr. C liked a lot of little courses, and those adapted from formal entertaining were a particularly special treat to him. If I did a palate cleanser of fresh sorbet before the meat course, or a fish course after the starter, or served salad after the main entrée, he was enchanted. Therefore, each party became a personal challenge, an opportunity to see if I could top what I had done previously. However, in trying to outdo myself, I once created a gorgeous menu for eight that just about did me in.

After platters of mixed hot hors d'oeuvres, I laid out a starter of chilled asparagus with hollandaise sauce, followed successively by individual moulds of salmon mousse, a palate cleanser of lemon sorbet in tiny cordial glasses, then succulent lamb loin chops, new potatoes, and a bouquetiere of baby vegetables, served al dente. I served a salad of mixed greens afterwards, followed by an impressive flourless chocolate pavé on a plate "painted" with raspberry coulis over a creme anglais sauce.

The problem with this lovely meal was that I had neglected to plan in advance what each course needed to be served *on*. Mr. C had full service for twelve in four different patterns of fine china; but I had eight guests, and my menu, unwisely, involved all the same plates: the starter and salad were served on salad plates; the salmon mousse on the dessert plate; and both the entrée and the dessert—because of the fancy "painting" of the plate—required the dinner plate. I had forgotten to factor in the necessity of washing each plate between courses.

Needless to say, after the entrée was served, the tempo of the dinner slowed dramatically, as I frantically washed plates to be used for the upcoming courses. Thereafter, I adapted my menus to suit the china on hand; for example, by planning a dessert or a starter that was served in a footed bowl.

Mr. Carstairs had happily adopted the European custom of eating late, after his very American cocktail hour. Even though dinner wasn't to be seated until 8 P.M., the biggest challenge I faced was learning to create meals that would hold successfully if delayed without being ruined, because they invariably had to be. Once in a great while, everyone arrived and went straight into the Jacuzzi, which was guaranteed to set the meal back. But mostly it was because his guests enjoyed Mr. C's hospitality and tended to prolong the happy hour by calling for another round.

The sheer amount of entertaining Mr. Carstairs did resulted in an interesting mélange of guests, yet those who dined at Promontory Point seemed to me far less diverse than some I remembered from the Maison du Gouverneur. He was a sociable man who met others easily and just as readily invited them to dinner. Complementing the assortment of business associates and friends from his college and military days were more recent acquaintances met on cruises or holidays, at football games, and through industry functions. In addition, he also had many high-placed contacts, so occasionally I would serve meals to Pentagon officials, high-ranking military personnel, and even television personalities. It is in these circumstances that many assume that a butler or other servant is at his most obsequious, yet I treated celebrities and dignitaries exactly as I treated everyone else. I've found that those who fawn on the rich, famous, or well born waste their time and destroy their own dignity; "sucking up" to someone is immediately obvious to the person of prominence, and is an insult to one's own self-respect.

"May I get you a drink, Mrs. Brandt? Vodka and soda with a lime?"

Mrs. Brandt was impressed. "Why, Christopher! You remember what I drink? But it must be nearly a year since we last saw Jack!"

Mrs. Brandt's reaction wasn't unique. During my tenure as a butler, many guests have asked me how I always remember what it is that they drink. Part of this is just good service training, to which any bartender will attest; things like memorizing what one's frequent customers drink makes for large

### Hints on Dealing With Inebriated Guests

If you do your own bartending when entertaining, you are probably grateful when guests offer to refresh their own drinks, rather than have you popping up constantly to refill someone's glass like a jack-in-the-box. However, unless you know your guests' habits very well, allowing your party free rein of your bar is a dangerous situation waiting to happen. Without someone keeping track of who has had what when, drinking can get out of control.

As a butler, I've had a lot of opportunity to practice the tactful circumvention of alcoholic overindulgence by guests. While I don't claim to have perfected it, the tips below have helped me to regulate the situations as much as possible.

*During cocktails:*

- Maintain control of your bar by insisting you do "the honors" of refreshing your guests' drinks.
- Have only one bottle of whatever liquor your guests are drinking visible in the bar.
- If a guest begins to show signs of tipsiness, decrease the percentage of alcohol in his drinks while increasing the mixer.
- If what he drinks is served straight, add more ice.

*At dinner:*

- Fill the inebriated guest's glass with slightly less wine than what is poured into the glasses of the other guests. This is an attempt to make the tipsy guest realize that he is drinking faster than everyone else, as he will likely empty his glass first.
- At the table, keep the wine bottle near you and do the pouring yourself. Be slow in pouring refills. When the glasses of others as well as the tipsy guest are empty, refill and top off the glasses of other guests, ending with yourself, so the bottle remains in your possession.

*(continued on next page)*

*(continued from previous page)*

*Afterwards:*

- Never let someone drive home if you feel they are intoxicated or in any way unsafe. (As a butler, I would bring the situation to the attention of the host and ask for permission to call a cab or take, or get the chauffeur to take, the guest home. In houses without staff the responsibility for attending to the needs of an inebriated guest is the host's; you must drive them home or offer a bed for the night.) *Do not take no for an answer.* It is preferable to have a guest who is insulted by the insinuation that he is incapacitated to one who incapacitates or kills himself or others.

tips. But in a butler's case, it goes beyond a drink. It reflects well on my employer when I know whether his guests drink their martinis shaken, rather than stirred, eat no red meat, or have an allergic reaction to milk products. I'm not blessed with anything more than an average memory. My secret weapon is called a butler's pantry book—although these days, I actually maintain it on computer.

I can't take credit for creating this invaluable tool; it has been used in some form by my forebears for generations. But I highly recommend it to present-day domestic servants, as well as to hosts and hostesses who don't employ live-in staff. The basic concept is simple—it is an entertainment diary. Into a butler's pantry book would go all of the above information, and much more. For every dinner party I served to Mr. Carstairs, I made a record of who was present, the menu, any substitutions I made in the recipes, and how the food was received. For example, when Mrs. Whittle hadn't eaten any of her brussels sprouts, I would make a note not to serve brussels sprouts to her again.

In fact, one of the reasons I kept the butler's pantry book was to guarantee that I did not serve Mr. Carstairs' guests the same meal twice. But it went beyond simple vanity. It was a means of ensuring that I didn't serve guests something that might cause them to break into hives, or worse, endanger their lives. I had once heard of an allergic reaction to something so obscure—the fumes a candle emits when extinguished—that the most careful of hosts might overlook it. I vowed never to allow such a slip-up to occur in any household that I ran.

How does one know whether their guests have allergies or food preferences? Very simply, one asks. Each dinner party that Mr. Carstairs requested, I would confirm by ringing each of the guests. This was not only a good way to introduce myself (it saved the "Wow, a real, live butler!" reaction at the door), but it allowed me an opportunity to make such enquiries.

"Now, Mrs. Smith, with regard to dinner; have you or Mr. Smith any allergies or food dislikes that I need take into account?" I'd ask. Occasionally this direct approach would startle people, and Mrs. Smith would assure me too quickly, "Oh, no, no; we're easy, we eat pretty much anything."

"Are you sure?" I'd press. "I don't want to make you something that you don't fancy. For example, I won't do a prime rib if you don't eat red meat, because even if you filled up on vegetables, you wouldn't enjoy your meal as much as you could."

"Oh . . . well, actually, I don't much care for fish. And Mr. Smith seems to have a touch of heartburn if there are green or red peppers in anything. But really, you can make us anything, and we're sure to enjoy it!"

In addition to its use as an entertainment tool, I used my butler's pantry book to keep track of many other items pertinent to Mr. Carstairs. I noted what he wore to both his own parties and important outside events. While I didn't lay out his everyday clothes as a true valet would have, I did make sure that he didn't wear easily recognizable clothing twice in the presence of the same people.

I kept track of the names of *maître d's* at his favorite restaurants to ensure good seats and especially attentive service. And there was a list of his favorite hotels—and preferred

## Sample Entry From Butler's Pantry Book

Date: March 11, 19XX

Dinner Party
Mrs. Weil's birthday

Mr. Carstairs (Grey trousers, white shirt, red plaid jumper, no tie; grey loafers)

Donna
Mr. and Mrs. Weil
Mr. Harrison and Ms. Crane
Mr. and Mrs. Whitcombe

KNOWN: (Culled from previous notes)

| | |
|---|---|
| Mr. Weil: | Vodka (Stolichnaya) with two stuffed olives (WATCH. Tendency to over-drink) |
| Mrs. Weil: | Chardonnay over ice. No tomatoes. |
| Mr. Harrison: | Scotch (Cutty Sark) and soda with a twist |
| Ms. Crane: | nondrinker. Diet Coke before, iced tea at dinner |
| Mr. Whitcombe: | Scotch (White Label), neat. Allergic to shellfish. |
| Mrs. Whitcombe: | White wine. No red meat. |

TABLE: Flowers: La Vonda (lavender-colored) roses in crystal rose bowl
China: Wedgwood Clio

MENU:

| | |
|---|---|
| Hors d'oeuvres | Herbed Couer à la Crème, Peppercorn Pâté with toast triangles and cornichons |
| Starter | Arugula Salad with Dijon Dressing |
| Main Course | Salmon with Apples, Pears, and Limes |
| | Brown Rice Milanese |
| | Green Beans with Mushrooms and Sesame Seeds |
| | Glazed Carrots |

Kendall Jackson Chardonnay "Vintners' Reserve" 19XX

Dessert Hazelnut Oeufs à la Neige

Notes: Lots of compliments on salmon. Dessert well-received —none left over—but colorless. Next time, find a more colorful presentation—perhaps use the accent plates or serve with a painted plate of raspberry purée and fresh cream.

rooms—in each of the many places he frequented on business and pleasure, so that when he wanted to go somewhere, I could arrange his accommodations and feel sure he would be comfortable.

The gifts he gave to people at Christmas or birthdays were noted so that he never made the mistake of giving the same thing to the same person twice. In addition, the book catalogued what was given to him, and by whom. In this way I could make sure the gift was discreetly on display or in use the next time that person visited the house. Favorite flowers of his friends' wives, if I learned of them, were noted so that they could be incorporated into the centerpiece the next time they dined at Promontory Point.

Special references were made to items like his and Donna's clothing; their shoe, dress, and ring sizes; her favorite perfume and that of each of his daughters; the type of chocolate his stepmother loved; what brand of golf ball his father preferred.

I also kept track of the birthdays of friends, relatives, and business acquaintances, but in Mr. Carstairs' case this was unnecessary. He himself kept a record of such things and never missed, nor was late, sending a handwritten card or note.

Keeping up such an elaborate butler's pantry book might take up to several hours every week, but the results, even those as simple as Mrs. Brandt's commendation, were well worth it. It boosted Mr. Carstairs' status as a thoughtful, accommodating host and mine as a true professional.

There was one party held at Promontory Point where my part in the show was simply to act as its coordinator. Always one to live life to the fullest, when Mr. Carstairs turned fifty, he wanted to celebrate in a big way. To that end he threw a black-tie birthday party for men only. There were fifty invited, and only one, on assignment in the Middle East, sent his regrets.

For this occasion Mr. C allowed me to have it professionally catered, with no expense spared. I was to organize everything, act as a host to the visiting staff to make sure they had what they needed, and make sure that the party flowed smoothly. In this case, in my best black tuxedo, I was dressed as the guests were.

After interviewing several of the top catering firms in Los Angeles, and talking to their references, I chose a medium-sized outfit with a sterling reputation. Together we worked to determine the menu, the decor, and the best set-up for the party, given the fact that it was to be held in February. I also arranged for entertainment and party favors for the guests.

The day before the party the tent was delivered and set up on the rear lawn overlooking the ocean. Over the thick grass they laid a sturdy full floor and a stage, and put up lights and heaters. Tables and chairs were delivered, and the crew set them up, going the extra step to make sure the tables were absolutely square and steady and didn't rock.

The professionalism of the catering staff when they arrived the afternoon of the party impressed me. Unused to overseeing a staff rather than pitching in and doing it myself, I watched fascinated as they deftly set up portable grills and steam tables in the garage, iced down the beer and wine, set the tables, and began to prepare the mounds of hors d'oeuvres. They brought absolutely everything: carving knives, serving utensils, towels and dish cloths, rubbish bins, even extension cords.

Outside under the tent, the tables were dressed to the nines. Everything was black and white. Floor-length black tablecloths were topped with starched white top cloths; large black napkins were folded elegantly into sparkling crystal wine glasses. Low floral arrangements of imported white flowers—hot house peonies, roses, spider mums, lilies, and snapdragons—filled gleaming silver bowls in the center of each table. The fine white china, all rented for the evening, had a band of gold on the rim. The party favors I had arranged, wrapped in iridescent silver-foiled paper and tied with black-and-white satin ribbons, graced each service plate.

At 7 P.M. the guests started to arrive. I greeted each

gentleman at the door and took his coat to my room, where I had the coat check set up. He was then directed to the bar, which opened off the butler's pantry, where a member of the catering staff was serving drinks. A second bar was set up outside, near the Jacuzzi, but the level of serving staff was such that a guest never had to approach it.

The din soon grew over the background music as the gentlemen talked and laughed. Drinks flowed freely, and the uniformed caterers passed hundreds of tasty morsels of meat, cheese, and shrimp. There was a general air of hilarity, of great expectations. They knew that because Mr. Carstairs was known to be outrageous, coupled with the fact that the party was stag, something exciting was going to happen. It had to be special.

And they weren't disappointed. In spite of its dress formality—the only accepted alternative to black tie was military dress uniform—the party was essentially a bachelor party, much like those which are held for the bridegroom before his wedding. Among other things, Mr. Carstairs had wanted me to arrange a handful of professional dancers to entertain at dinner and cavort with the men the rest of the evening.

The ladies had arrived at half-past six, and I'd shown them into the guest room. While the men enjoyed the cocktail hour, I brought a plate of hors d'oeuvres in to where they were relaxing before their scheduled performance.

"Come in," a female voice called, in answer to my knock.

I must have interrupted them as they changed, because all six of them were in some form of undress. "Uh ... some canapés, ladies?" I asked, keeping my eyes on their faces.

Returning to the party, I did a quick once-over to see that everything seemed to be in order. Then, at the high-sign from the catering chef, I stepped up onto the stage and cleared my throat theatrically.

"My lords, ladies—ahem; strike that!—and gentlemen—dinner is served."

There was some laughter and scattered applause as the men began to make their way toward the tables and milled around the chairs. I led as many as possible to their assigned seats. Shouts of laughter, catcalls, and comments abounded as they opened their party favors.

For each gentleman I had had a racing car driver-style white silk scarf monogrammed with his initials and the date of the party. But in a lighter vein, each also had a small plastic box filled with colored prophylactics. "Life insurance for the next fifty years," the enclosed card read.

A feeling of *déjà vu* came over me as I watched the waiters begin to serve the first course of Maryland crab cakes with sauce remoulade. It was almost as though I were back in my restaurant days, only now I was the *maître d'*.

One gentleman, intent on using the loo before the meal began, stopped as he came abreast of me.

"Chris, help me out," he said in a low voice. "There must be fifty pieces of cutlery in front of my place. How do I know which one to use?"

There were actually only seven pieces of silverware per place setting, but I nodded seriously. "Just remember, sir, outside-in."

"Outside-in. Okay. Thanks." He winked conspiratorially and, clapping me on the shoulder, continued on his quest.

The meal went off without a hitch. A palate cleanser of mango sorbet followed the crab cakes, before a main course consisting of sixteen-ounce Porterhouse steaks, twice-baked jacket potatoes, and masses of fresh vegetables. A simple salad of winter greens followed the main course. Throughout the dinner various guests took the stage and made speeches, or more accurately, tossed jibes in honor of Mr. Carstairs' birthday. But when dessert was ready to be presented, I asked for everyone's attention.

From the house the waiters appeared in a line, each wheeling a *guéridon*. From its compartment, each brought forth dessert plates of french vanilla ice cream rolled up in crepes and placed them in front of the dinner guests. Then in unison they proceeded to put the finishing touches to the large sauté pan of Cherries Jubilee on the burner, then ignite the brandy.

*Whoosh!* There was a little roar as nine separate pans were flambéed, all at once. The effect was spectacular. As the waiters moved around the table, dishing the cherry mixture over the crepes, there was a burst of spontaneous applause.

While they ate dessert, the music emanating from the big sound system changed from unobtrusive background music to a bumping, gyrating beat. There were hoots of surprise and delight as, from the side of the house, the dancers shimmied to the stage. Although they came out fully clothed, what remained when they had finished their act didn't leave a lot to the imagination.

Afterwards the ladies changed into evening wear and dancing and drinking continued into the wee hours in the living room. At 1 A.M., after the caterers had finished packing up, I received permission to depart, knowing I would need to be up early the next morning. In addition to those guests from out of town who were staying at the house, Mr. Vanders had offered his guest quarters to a number of Mr. Carstairs' visitors, so I figured I'd have about six for breakfast.

The following morning, as I surveyed the detritus of a good time presumably had by all, I was glad I had scheduled a special cleaning session with Sheilah. I was also glad I had thought to lay in lots of breakfast supplies, because everywhere I looked, I saw bodies crashed out—on couches, in chairs, on rugs, on chaise longues on the patio, everywhere. For hours afterwards, people stumbled out of the woodwork.

"Why, good morning, Colonel Barry! Where on earth did you sleep, sir?"

"I dunno; it wasn't very comfortable, though. I think it was on the coffee table in the den."

Discretion is a word almost synonymous with butlers, and it's true one doesn't progress to professional status without learning to keep one's mouth closed and one's thoughts to oneself. The ability to do so stood me in good stead when I worked for Mr. Carstairs. His divorce final, he remained true to the declaration he had made to me in Monte Carlo—life was too short; he was going to enjoy himself.

Mr. Carstairs had a combination that made him irresistible to many women—an intensely magnetic personality, good looks, and lots of money. In addition to his rather dashing, Sean Connery-like looks, there was something incredibly virile about him. In spite of his height, his movements were lithe and fluid, his walk graceful even in cowboy boots. He kept deeply tanned and very fit. Further, he had a way of looking women over, eyebrows raised speculatively over his surprisingly light eyes that seemed only to intrigue them more. Women were soon hooked by his charm, failing to see that, truthfully, he sometimes treated them rather chauvinistically.

It is a point of pride in my trade that one must not slip with the wrong name. But under the circumstances, it was safer to avoid the consequences of a possible error, so with some relief, I retreated behind the butler's ubiquitous "Madame."

But if Mr. C kept his options open, some of his mates were downright libidinous. Whether it was coincidental or a result of a cycle in their lives, a number of the men in his circle had also divorced. Knowing Mr. C to be up for anything, a "comrade in arms," so to speak, he received frequent calls to go out and play. Every so often I acted as chauffeur for a night of pub-crawling (which, for better or worse, usually included Donna). On these occasions his mates would plan on staying the night at Promontory Point regardless of whether or not they "got lucky." This was a relief, as it saved me having to take each of them to their far-flung homes after what was always a late night.

The sort of pubs Mr. C and his friends preferred were dance bars, often country-western ones, and we would often make the circuit of two or three before the night's end. Somewhere along the route his mates would each have met a lady friend. I was rather impressed by this; it was rare that these men failed to find a companion, although I'm sure the mention of having a private limousine waiting couldn't help but make a nice pick-up line. Whomever they met usually came back to the house with them, and either the men or myself would take them back to their cars the following morning.

Once, however, an hour after I had brought Mr. Carstairs, Donna, his two friends, and their dates back to Promontory Point and gone to bed, Mr. C woke me up.

"Chris?"

"Hmmmphh?" Sleepily I stumbled out of bed, struggled into my dressing gown, and went to the door.

"Sorry, slight problem here. One of the girls wants to go home. The one Dick's with. Can you run her back?"

As I redressed quickly, I checked my watch: quarter to three. With a yawn I hoped she had driven herself to the bar so that I could drop her there. But I wasn't to be so lucky. Her name was Pamela, she told me, and she had gone to the bar with some girlfriends. Could I take her home? She named a town some twenty-five miles away. With a sigh, I turned up the radio to help keep myself awake, and started to activate the privacy shield that separated the driver's quarters from the passenger section.

"Oh, don't do that, will you?" she said. "It's awful lonely back here by myself"

Something in her voice made me wonder why she hadn't stayed with Dick in the first place. "There's a television in the cupboard to your left, ma'am," I told her helpfully.

"Does it get dirty movies?" she asked coyly, confirming my suspicions.

"I've no idea, madame," I said, going ultraformal.

She giggled, and I heard her fix herself a drink from the bar as she flipped through the stations. Surreptitiously watching the side mirrors for signs of the highway patrol, I sped up gradually. It couldn't be too much farther now.

From the back seat, something soft sailed by my ear and landed in my lap. Momentarily taking my eyes from the road, I looked down.

There were her panties.

Peals of laughter rang out from the passenger section as the back of my neck went fiery red. I found my voice.

"Madame, I really must ask you to keep your belongings to yourself. It impairs my ability to drive—"

"Then don't drive," she said softly. Her breath was warm on my neck. I could see in the rear-view mirror she had moved to the jump seat, which backed up against the driver's section. Her skirt was pushed up to her waist and her blouse was unbuttoned. "Pull off at the next off-ramp and park . . . and come back here with me."

My hands were clammy. I tried to put some authority in my tone. "Madame, this is *most* improper. Please confine your conversation to directing me to where you wish to be taken. There is a telephone on your right that will allow you to communicate with me." With that, I raised the darkened privacy shield, shutting out her amused laughter.

When we finally reached her house, I left the engine running as I came round to open the car door for her. For a moment she smiled at me invitingly, not moving, her blouse still open. Then, seeing that I wasn't going to crawl into the back of the car with her, she sighed and got out.

"Good night, Christopher," she said. "Sure you don't want to come in for a nightcap?"

"Good night, madame," I said, closing the car door. Without another word I got back into the car and drove away.

The next morning when I cleaned out the car, I found her billfold, left rather artfully on the corner of the seat cushion. A modern-day dropped handkerchief for me to return? I wasn't accepting the offer. I posted the billfold (and her panties) back to her by Federal Express, putting the country-western bar as the return address.

With the rather flamboyant exception of *Lady Chatterley's Lover*, propositioning a manservant in uniform is not a common occurrence. Yet after a while in the States, I noticed a curious thing—among some people there seemed to be a secret game called Get the Butler to Drop his Jaw.

In Jeeves's day no one would have paid any attention to me, much less tried to see if they could shock or embarrass me. Whether it was because a butler was such an oddity among Mr. Carstairs' set, a reaction to the well-known British reserve, or basic curiosity, I couldn't quite fathom. But with some regularity something happened that I suspected had been engineered to make me drop my composure. One of the biggest players of this game seemed to be Mr. Buffulo.

Mr. Carstairs had issued an open invitation to his many friends to visit Promontory Point, regardless of whether he was in residence. Although a lot of visitors took him up on the offer when he was there, it seemed to me that even more took advantage of his hospitality by visiting when he was away. I suspected that Promontory Point was considered a sort of retreat, a scene for a rendezvous by some of his friends, and not always just the divorced ones. Regardless, my instructions from Mr. Carstairs were to take care of his guests as I would of him.

One such visitor was Mr. Buffulo, an old high school chum of Mr. Carstairs. A large, florid man with a loud voice and a rather coarse sense of humor, Mr. Buffulo visited a couple of times each year, almost always when Mr. Carstairs was elsewhere. I had a deep suspicion Mr. C preferred it that way.

Mr. Buffulo made full use of Promontory Point's facilities during his visits, not the least of which were my services. He loved playing Lord of the Manor, and wanted a full breakfast served to him in bed each morning at eight, and a lunch packed for him to take down to the beach by ten. Fortunately I rarely had to fix him dinner, as Mr. Buffulo spent his evenings out on the prowl. His favorite haunts were the topless places down near the airport.

Remaining calm and unruffled is part of the job. But on occasion Mr. Buffulo's crassness put my impassivity to the test.

I went on duty at my customary 7 A.M., making a tour of the premises and straightening anything that had been mussed up since the previous evening. One morning, after I had picked up no less than four oversized bathing towels from where they lay in damp heaps near the Jacuzzi, I carried the breakfast that he had requested the previous evening down to the guest room. As usual, it was a substantial start for the day: three eggs, scrambled with cheddar cheese, four pieces of well-done bacon, four pieces of toast with butter and preserves, coffee, and fresh-squeezed orange juice. I knocked at the door.

"Sir? Your breakfast."

There was no answer. Balancing the laden bed tray on one arm, I tried the door. It opened readily, but Mr. Buffulo wasn't there, and the bed showed no signs of having been slept in. I was puzzled and a little annoyed. The man had never stayed out all night before, but if he had decided to do so, I wish he had rung and left me a message before I prepared this whole spread.

I started back to the kitchen when I suddenly had a horrible thought. Surely he hadn't decided to sleep in Mr. Carstairs' room? As generous as Mr. C was, he did not like people using his room unless the number of guests at one time made it unavoidable. Still carrying the tray, I went down the hall to the master bedroom and knocked once again.

"Yeah, come on in," Mr. Buffulo answered my enquiry.

Inwardly disgusted, I opened the door. Maneuvering my full tray, I started for the bed, when I became aware that Mr. Buffulo wasn't the only one in it. Snuggled next to his large form was a naked shoulder and a mass of bleached blonde hair. A female face, much made up but somewhat smeared now, raised itself from the pillow and regarded me sleepily.

One mustn't show any form of surprise or embarrassment, I reminded myself, to find an unknown female in bed with your employer—or his guests, as the case may be. Carefully making my face blank, I spoke to Mr. Buffulo.

"Will the lady have breakfast as well?"

Incidentally, decorum dictates that such a guest is addressed as a lady—even when the situation makes the title seem ludicrously inaccurate.

The breakfast incident wasn't the only time that antics of Mr. Buffulo's had put me on the spot, and I began to suspect that he made it a personal quest to try to shake my composure. On one visit he brought a female guest whom he introduced simply as Brandi. With a companion, he didn't need to frequent the men's bars, with the result that I wound up doing dinner for them in addition to breakfast and lunch, as well as serving them endless drinks as they sunbathed—nude—by the pool.

The corker, however, came one evening when they were in the Jacuzzi. I was in the kitchen, putting the finishing touches to the washing-up of the dinner I had served them earlier, when I heard Mr. Buffulo call from the patio. His loud voice was clearly audible through the open window on the balmy night air.

"Hey, Chris? Could you get us a couple of rum and cokes?"

"Certainly, sir," I said.

I stepped out on the patio a few minutes later with the drinks on a tray. Mr. Buffulo, his beefy arms draped on the Jacuzzi's edge, was apparently alone in the Jacuzzi. His head was thrown back, his eyes shut, and a beatific smile lighted his flushed face.

As I neared, however, I saw I was mistaken. There was a profusion of bubbles rising from his lap.

Mr. Buffulo opened his eyes and winked at me.

"Scuba training," he said smugly. "Good, isn't she?"

I set the drinks down on the deck next to him. "I'm afraid tomorrow's my day off, sir," I said formally. "Will there be anything else this evening, before I go?"

# 12

# Contract Butlering

The clock in the living room was just striking eleven as I came in the front door, but Kim was still up, engrossed in a book.

"Hi," she said, as I leaned over to give her a quick kiss. We had gotten married the previous autumn—three years, almost to the day, from the day I had come to America.

She put down her book. "Bad night?"

"No, just a long day," I said, collapsing onto the sofa. Even though I was exhausted to the point of dropping, the sight of her and the cozy room cheered me. For it was *home.* After nearly fifteen years of living in other people's houses, of possessing only what I could easily carry with me, the pride of ownership was unbelievable.

I sat for some minutes with eyes closed, thinking. There was something bothering me that we needed to discuss, but I didn't have all the answers to the questions that I knew would inevitably follow. But with a sigh, I took the plunge.

"It's time for a change," I said.

"Yeah?" Kim enquired, reaching for my hand. "Why's that?"

"It's the job," I said. "Mr. C's a good boss, generally

speaking. But I've gone as far as I can go with him. The day-to-day work of managing the house and doing the dinner parties I can do in my sleep. I need more stimulation."

"You mean chopping down a dozen oak trees doesn't stimulate you?" she asked drily, referring to one of my more recent "projects"—four days spent clearing a plot of Mr. Carstairs' land. Not too surprisingly, my muscles had ached for days afterwards; felling trees wasn't generally in a majordomo's job description.

Her comment wasn't without truth, though. Over the past few months there had been many such departures; in fact, of late it seemed my already broad job description read more like a general contractor than someone in private service. In addition to helping to redesign, then overseeing a complete renovation of his kitchen and butler's pantry, I had undertaken such ventures as laying an industrial tile floor in one of his company's bathrooms, repainting his suite of offices, and replacing the sub-flooring and wall paneling in a conference room.

"Actually, yes it does," I told Kim, referring to the question of stimulation. "I've volunteered for projects like that because I enjoy learning new skills. At the end of the day there's a sense of accomplishment because I've achieved something new, something novel—even if it's way off the list of things that a majordomo might do. But the problem is, they're just that—projects. And projects end.

"And that's the point. Because as far as 'what I should do,' he's not going to buy a castle in France or a sprawling mansion in Newport, Rhode Island, where I can move up to being responsible for overseeing a large staff. There's no opportunity for advancement, no matter how much time I put in. And, frankly, the eighty-hour weeks are getting me down."

"It shows," she said. "You usually jump out of bed in the morning before the alarm even goes off. But lately I've seen you turn it off and go back to sleep. You're not happy anymore."

"Well, maybe I'll feel better after our holiday next week."

Able to travel now that I had been granted legal residency in the United States, Kim and I were taking a trip back to England. "When we get back home, let's see how I feel, and decide what to do from there."

"Going home" to England was more of a symbolic gesture than a sentimental one, for I knew now that I would never return to live there. I loved young, vibrant, dynamic America. My house in England I regarded as the Investment, rather than a potential residence, even part-time. That investment, however, was to prove critical in determining my eventual course of action.

My brother had insisted that we stay with him during our holiday, for which I was grateful; I knew, in spite of the Home Help that came in once a week to "do" for my widowed father, the old house wouldn't be in any shape for "company" to stay. Still, we wanted to visit, and Kim in particular wanted to see the Investment she had heard so much about.

Although my father assured me each month when I sent the money for the bills that the house was fine, I wasn't so sure. A house of that age took maintenance. I also had a sneaking hunch that, in a misguided effort to save me money, he played down the problems of which I did learn. I calculated that I might have to do some repairs while we were there. So within a few hours of our arrival, we paid an unannounced call on my father in West London.

The house was a disaster.

Grasses and thistles stood nearly three feet tall in the front garden, and weeds infiltrated the once-smart mosaic tile pathway. In the hallway, wallpaper stained dark from the rising damp, peeled from the wall and ceiling. A ridge peak tile had come loose from the roof and crashed through the corrugated plastic roof of the attached conservatory. Because it had been cheaply and inexpertly mended, mould grew down the interior wall where the water still leaked in.

Needless to say, the contrast to the pristine residences I had occupied over the past fifteen years was extreme.

My elderly father, stubborn and set in his ways, had lived

there too long to notice anything amiss. "What? It's fine. It's good enough for me," he argued when I protested.

"It's not fine! The house needs insulating—damp coursing —the bricks need to be remortared—the roof needs to be done. And what on earth happened to the conservatory? Dad, I've got to get someone out here to do it. This place is falling apart!"

"No! This is my home. I live here, not you, and I want it left as it is. I don't want people in and out of my house. They interrupt me and get in my way. I want to be left alone."

He glared at me balefully as we faced each other across the once-familiar sitting room. We had never fought, never shouted before. I had to leave. My eyes were streaming and I knew it wasn't wholly due to allergies.

Shell-shocked by the state of the Investment, Kim and I found the rest of our holiday spoiled. With the experience borne of my newfound construction skills, I estimated with horror that it would require tens of thousands of dollars in order to bring the house back to salable condition. Even with our two incomes, that sort of ready capital was beyond our reach, particularly when we had just sunk every bit of savings we had into the purchase of our own house.

Now I *had* to make more money—much more. And unfortunately I knew I couldn't do so working for my current employer.

Within a week of our return from England, I approached Mr. Carstairs about my career prospects. His answers confirmed that he had no residential aspirations beyond Promontory Point and regardless of what further responsibilities I might undertake for him, I had essentially reached the peak of my earnings potential in his employ. Working the hours I averaged when he was in residence, there was no chance of my taking on a second job. Reluctantly I concluded that, without opportunity for meaningful job growth and salary increase, there was nowhere further for me to go with him. Accordingly, I submitted my resignation.

Mr. Carstairs was not exactly wild about my decision, but after considerable discussion over the next few days he saw that, given our different goals, my continued employment would be futile. However, as I didn't want to leave him in the lurch, I gave five months' notice, during which time I agreed I would find, hire, and train my replacement.

"Now, with all due respect sir, I'm not going to be able to find someone who will do everything that I currently do for you for the same salary, much less the reduced one you've authorized."

In the intervening days since my announcement, Mr. Carstairs had begun to look at the situation from his usual businesslike perspective. "I realize that, and believe me, I don't want an endless turnover of staff like there is at the Whitfields'. I've been giving the matter a lot of thought, and this is what I see: Okay, I understand why you want to leave. You've got a lot of get-up-and-go, and you want to move up. Fair enough, except I can't offer that here. Frankly, what I need is someone who is happy to have mastered his job, and having done so, doesn't feel the need to move on to something bigger. Someone who doesn't have an exterior life or family responsibilities, and therefore can concentrate one hundred percent on looking after me."

Unfortunately, in spite of my best efforts over the next five months, I couldn't find him that paragon of servility. In the end, with much frustration I settled for someone who had no formal domestic training, but seemed to have the right attitude—the willingness to learn and do whatever Mr. Carstairs needed. I wasn't overjoyed with my replacement, but I had exhausted my resources under the stipulations given.

It was with substantial regret that I approached Mr. Carstairs on my final day to say goodbye.

"Best of luck, Chris," he said, with the broad smile I had come to know so well since our interview, so many years before. "Anything you need from me—a reference, information, whatever—or anything I can do, just call. You know where I'll be." He offered his hand and I shook it warmly. Then, with a final salute, I left the keys to the Pontiac on the counter, took the envelope that contained my final paycheck, and walked out the front door to where Kim was waiting to drive me home. When I opened the envelope later, I found he had added a substantial gratuity.

"Can you take an interview tomorrow at eleven?" the placement agent asked. "In Los Angeles?"

"Certainly, madame. Am I permitted to know who it is?"

"Well, actually it's—" She named a flamboyant young film star, whom I'll refer to as Miss Dale.

"And she wants a *butler*?" From what I had read of Miss Dale and her lifestyle, this seemed remarkable.

"Well, yeah, in a loose sense of the word. Actually I think you'd find it to be a little bit of everything."

"Have you spoken to them about me? Do they know my qualifications?" I queried. "I've told you what sort of a position I'm looking for. Do you see it as a good match?"

"Of course I have, sweetheart. And I've told them what a doll you are. I'm sure they'll just *love* you."

The house in the Hollywood hills was squarish and unremarkable and, surprisingly, without a guard gate of any sort. Perhaps Miss Dale had a cotillion of body guards in lieu of a security system.

I was shown into a bright, rather unfriendly room, the most remarkable features of which were garish canvasses of modern art on the walls and a preponderance of popcorn kernels all over the carpet.

A woman in her late twenties, thin to the point of anorexia, banged into the room from the hall. She was dressed in a pair of skin-tight black pants, cowboy boots, and a long black tunic, and her blonde hair was in dire need of a touch-up at the roots. She introduced herself as Sandra, Miss Dale's friend and personal secretary, and explained that she was doing the interviews. "Sit down, won't you?"

I brushed some stray pieces of crushed popcorn from a modern chair that looked more like an agricultural combine.

"Oh, Miss Dale *loves* popcorn. It's her passion," Sandra said, with an airy wave.

She gave only a cursory glance at the c.v. I handed her,

and launched straight into a rambling description of my job duties.

"Miss Dale, as you know, is going through a divorce right now, and she really needs to feel loved and supported. She likes to get out and party to make herself feel better."

"I see," I murmured, though in truth, I didn't see.

"She really needs someone to take care of her—make her meals, do her shopping, take care of her house, do her laundry, travel with her, that sort of thing. Basically, you'd be with her all the time, going where she goes, watching out for her, so of course you'd have to live here. Where did you say you live now?"

"We live in Orange Cou—"'

"We?" She seemed slightly puzzled.

"My wife and I."

"You're *married*? But we told the agency that we wanted someone g— that is, I mean, wouldn't your wife be a little jealous of you spending all your time with Miss Dale?"

"Madame," I said formally, "this is my *profession.* My wife knows she has no cause for jealousy."

"But—but we really want someone who can be available for Miss Dale twenty-four hours a day, seven days a week."

I rose and picked up my briefcase. "In that case, I'm terribly sorry to have wasted your time. It seems you don't want a butler, you want a slave. Good day."

Self-employment, I thought, would allow me more opportunities than those afforded by working for someone else. And, still with a bad taste in my mouth from the fruitless interviews arranged by placement counselors who simply wanted to place a body, any body, in a job so that they could collect their commission, I had an idea.

Having just gone through the lengthy hiring process in replacing myself, I knew how important it was that the needs of an employer and their prospective employee match. Further, few agencies in the country dealt in the placement of the high end of the servant spectrum—butlers, chefs, majordomos, and the like. Who would better know the ins and outs of professional domestic staff than someone who had been there? I could become an agency in my own right, concentrating on matching only high-level staff—no *au pairs* or house cleaners—with suitable employers.

I set up a business that I called English Domestic Services and placed ads in the Yellow Pages. Thinking I could begin building my file of possible staff with those I already knew, I started networking to find out who was leaving, who was hiring, and who might need my services.

I had been in business only a couple of months when I got a phone call from a reporter at the *Los Angeles Times*. She was, she said, doing an article on entertaining and my business name had intrigued her. What, exactly, did I do?

When I told her I matched high-level domestic staff to appropriate households, she interrupted me.

"Do you provide butlers for hire, say, for a party?"

"Certainly, madame," I said immediately. Truthfully, I had never thought of it, but what a wonderful idea. If someone needed a butler for one night, I could do that. I had moonlighted occasionally for Mr. Vanders for five years, and still did so.

Our subsequent interview appeared as part of a larger article on "elegant touches that made a party special," and within two weeks of its publication I had lined up four jobs as a contract butler.

Contract butlering offered those without staff the cachet of a butler in full black tie for a special occasion. People were charmed with the idea, and I began to get referrals and repeat business.

One of the most elegant parties I ever served was at the home of a gentleman called Dr. Garnham. His was one of the most beautifully decorated homes I had seen since I had come to the States, and when his guests arrived, I knew why. This was a crowd of art connoisseurs, collectors, and interior designers. Evident everywhere in Dr. Garnham's small, but stunning oceanview home were examples of his exquisite taste in artwork, collectibles, and *objets d'art.* Highlighting the sun-filled rooms were large vases filled with graceful white calla lilies for an effect both simple and elegant.

As I did for all of my contract butler engagements, I had brought my collection of polished silverplate serving trays to use. This I considered to be part of the package—an English butler in a crisp black tuxedo with a silver tray. But in this gentleman's case, it was unnecessary. Showing me to a large cupboard near the formal dining room, he opened the doors to reveal perhaps two dozen trays, each carefully wrapped in tarnish-proof cloth. As I brought them forth, I was surprised, in a house of this size, to find Dr. Garnham's ornate trays were real sterling silver. And they weighed a ton. Accustomed as I was to carrying trays, I knew my arms would ache by the time I got home.

That the party had a theme was evident in the way the table was laid. Set with understated Lenox china over a black tablecloth, it was decorated in the intentionally garish colors of New Orleans' Mardi Gras celebration. Confetti, chocolate doubloons, strands of *faux* pearls, and bright beads were scattered the length of the table; and the napkins, folded into wine glasses, were in bright hues of crimson red, lemon yellow, royal blue, orange, and purple. A Susan B. Anthony silver dollar was taped under each plate; it was, Dr. Garnham explained, a symbol of good luck. The music that was piped over the omnipresent sound system was traditional Dixieland jazz, and the food, all New Orleans specialties—Cajun-seasoned crawfish, dirty rice, baked bananas in rum, black-eyed peas and sausage and gumbo, which guests washed down with a tropical-style-drink called a Hurricane. The twenty guests laughed and joked, and offered repeated toasts to an apparently absent guest named Phillip.

I found out afterwards that it had been a wake.

"Phillip loved New Orleans," Dr. Garnham explained, as I prepared to depart. "He loved its bigger-than-life gaiety, its Southern charm and grace with the element of seediness underneath. And he especially loved the idea of the traditional black Dixieland funeral. What happens is, the jazz band and the mourners all walk behind the horse-drawn coffin to the cemetery, and the whole way the band plays spirituals. But, because they believe that the dead have gone to a better life then that found on earth, the music played as they return from the burial is exuberant, even joyful. Phillip always felt *that* was the spirit in which a funeral should be held."

At first my jobs were simply butlering: greeting, serving drinks, hors d'oeuvres, announcing dinner and serving it, pouring wine, tidying up afterwards. But after a month or so, when the size of the parties were within my manageability, I offered to do the cooking of the meal as well, so that the client could truly be a guest at his or her own party.

For these events, the clients and I would discuss the menu, then determine what was needed to create it both from a food and a cooking and serving-ware standpoint. I would visit their homes, do an inventory of their equipment, and offer to do the shopping for them if they wished, but as they were paying me by the hour, most clients preferred to do their own. On the day of the party, I would arrive in the afternoon, set the table and prep the food as far as possible, then handle the party much as I had done for Mr. Carstairs for years. Not only was I paid my stated hourly rate, but my clients often added a generous cash tip. Even more gratifying, I often had at least one other referral from the event.

I found that one of the engagements I was most often called to do were cocktail parties. These were a personal favorite of mine, and whenever possible, I tried to provide the food as well as the service. More so than any other type of party, the fare of a cocktail party offers the most creative opportunities for the cook, as an endless number of canapés and other highly decorative finger foods fall under the label "appetizers." In spite of the time-consuming, painstaking, often repetitive work, I loved the challenge of creating gorgeous bite-sized morsels.

Many of my clients saw the advantage of this and commissioned me to do both food and service, but occasionally I came across someone who preferred to do all the food preparation themselves. Such a client was Mrs. Farrell, who was planning an old-fashioned winter wassail party.

"No, that's okay, Christopher, I have it all under control. I have *a fabulous* cookbook with the most *marvelous* ideas in it. I can't *wait* to try some of them!"

"You haven't tried the recipes before, madame?" This was not a good sign.

"No, but they're *terribly* simple—you'll see. There's this lovely one made with chopped eggs and Belgian endive, and this idea for skewered tortellini, and cherry tomatoes filled with crab salad, and apples with chicken liver pâté piped on them, and—"

I was getting nervous. Some of the hors d'oeuvres she had just mentioned were fairly time-consuming to put together. I offered again to help with her menu, suggesting that she intersperse some of her extravagant hors d'oeuvres ideas with others that could be prepared in advance, but she was adamant.

"I'm *fine,* don't worry. You just come all dolled up in your tux and your accent!"

Still, she continued to call and ask my opinions about various aspects of her proposed party. People would be bringing some things, she explained; she would need them set out immediately so that the guest would see that their dish was welcome. She wanted me to serve wassail (a hot, spiced, liquor-infused apple cider) to the arriving guests as I took their coats. No, wassail wasn't the only thing to be served. There was to be beer and wine and champagne as well. And coffee.

Even if I was just to serve the party, forty people were too many to serve without someone backing me up in the kitchen, plating the hors d'oeuvres and decorating the platters, concocting the wassail and keeping it warm, keeping things orderly and as clean as possible. After three conversations Mrs. Farrell yielded and allowed me to bring in Kim to help. And, as the days ticked off closer to her party, she agreed to our coming two hours earlier than we otherwise

### The Art of Presentation

"Presentation" refers to the position of food on the plate—the way the table is set, the way the wine is served, the meal offered as almost a theatrical event. Actually there is quite a lot of similarity to the theater. The timing, needed to orchestrate the simultaneous finish of the meal components, is the choreography; your table, the backdrop; your plate, the stage. Ensuring that your dish is as visually appealing as possible is important, because as professionals know, we eat with our eyes more than we do with our tastebuds. As they say in the food service industry, presentation is everything.

Of course in the perfect world you would have the time to make the wonderful edible garnishes that adorn plates in fine restaurants. But in most cases a menu chosen for its colors and textures, such as the example given on page 155 in the Butler's Pantry Book, will give you all the presentation you need, allowing you to save your decorative efforts for the dessert. Still, here are five simple plate garnishes that take little time or artistic talent, yet manage to imply that you've spent some time training in a fine culinary school somewhere.

- *Citrus twists.* For seafood, veal piccata, or meals with a citrus fruit-based sauce, I prefer to use both a lemon and a lime. Slice the lemon thinly, then make a cut from the peel to the center of the fruit. Holding the slice on either side of the cut, twist in opposite directions and set on plate. For the lemon-lime version, place lime on top of lemon, cuts aligned, and twist together.
- *Green onion brushes.* Especially nice atop white rice served with oriental-style food, or those with teriyaki sauces. Wash green onions and cut off root and most of the top, then cut into two or three pieces. With a sharp knife, make a cut halfway down into the onion (don't cut all the way, or the brush won't hold together), then roll the onion a quarter turn and make a cut of equal depth. Make at least six cuts

*(continued on next page)*

*(continued from previous page)*

into the top of the onion piece. Drop the cut onion into ice water and allow to chill thirty minutes; the onion will open and curl back on itself slightly. (For Mexican or south-of-the border food, a red chili pepper—either a small one or the top of a long thin one—can be prepared in the same way. Wear gloves when handling chilis, and avoid touching your face!)

- *Carrot Bundles.* Peel and cut a few tender young carrots into three-inch-long fine matchsticks. Drop into boiling water to blanch for thirty seconds (this heightens the color). For the ties, cut the root from a green onion and discard. Soften the tops by pouring boiling water over it. Drain and rinse in cold water, then cut lengthwise into narrow strips. Take a bundle of matchstick carrots and wrap with the green onion, finishing with a half-knot. Serve hot as a vegetable or cold as a garnish.
- *Zucchini fans.* Use a small zucchini, no larger than five to six inches. Blanch in boiling water for two or three minutes, remove and plunge into cold water to arrest the cooking process and set the color. Cut the ends off the zucchini, halve crosswise, then cut each half lengthwise (creating four pieces). Place on cutting board, with green skin facing you. Leaving one half-inch at the top, use a sharp knife to make very fine comb-like vertical slices down the length of the zucchini. Gently pressing the zucchini flat with the back of the knife will make the fine slices fan out.
- *Lemon basket.* This looks particularly nice as a decoration to a seafood platter. Use a smooth, unblemished lemon and place it on its side on a cutting board. Approximately in the middle, make two parallel cuts about ⅜" apart halfway through the lemon to form the handle. From the stem, slice horizontally to the first cut and remove the wedge. Repeat on the other side. Carefully cut away the flesh from the underside of the handle and interior of the lemon to finish the basket. Fill with fresh herbs such as parsley, dill, thyme, or marjoram.

would have, in case there was some final preparation she needed handled.

On the morning of the party a frazzled Mrs. Farrell, still in her housecoat, met us at the door. Looking over her shoulder, I was glad we had come early. I could see that the dining table in the room beyond was far from ready; it still had the debris that every household collects—piles of bills, magazines to be read, odds and ends from the shopping waiting to be taken to another part of the house. A heap of assorted serving trays and baskets were the only indication of pre-party planning evident.

The tiny apartment consisted of four rooms on the lower level, with bedrooms upstairs. The entire place was cluttered with lovely, ornate furniture. I wondered how it would hold forty guests.

Stopping us in the hall, Mrs. Farrell said: "Now, Christopher, what I picture is this. You greet the guests here, take their coats, and hand them a cup of hot wassail, dressed with a little cinnamon stick, before they continue into the party."

As she spoke, I did some rapid calculations. This was going to be difficult at best. In the narrow hallway was a small antique table that really ought to be moved to accommodate the flow of traffic. But without it, I had no place for the wassail. Further, the only place for coats was an upstairs bedroom. I would need more hands than I had in order to juggle the coats of arriving guests, pour and hand them a cup of steaming wassail from the tiny, intrusive table, direct them into the party, then run upstairs and drop their coats. If more than two guests arrived at a time, it would be a nightmare.

I explained the logistics problem to Mrs. Farrell. A little disappointed, she agreed to a compromise; I would bring the guests a cup of wassail as soon as I had gotten rid of their coats. The only problem with this was that I still had to be in two places at once—the front door, and the dining room, serving wassail.

Having reached an agreement, we proceeded toward the kitchen. The sight that greeted our eyes on arrival made us

## Notes for Successful Cocktail Parties

Cocktail parties differ from other parties in that they're generally of shorter duration—say, two hours, with the unwritten expectation that guests will go on to dinner elsewhere. In the following tips I differentiate between a cocktail party and a cocktail hour, where a dinner is to follow, as they have distinctly different purposes.

*Food*

- A canapé differs from an hors d'oeuvre in that the former always has an element of bread in it as presented, often resembling a small tea sandwich or filled savory pastry. An hors d'oeuvre can stand alone, or be added to a cracker, toast round, or other "carrier." (The literal translation of hors d'oeuvre is "outside the main works," or "not of the main preparation.")
- Hors d'oeuvres are generally rich in fat, for a purpose—fat buffers the impact of alcohol. Some good choices for cocktail parties include caviar, pâtés, terrines, and stuffed or marinated vegetables, such as stuffed mushroom caps.
- Always serve lots of canapés and hors d'oeuvres at cocktail parties, and make them substantial in order to offset the alcohol as much as possible. Plan on eight to ten pieces per person, slightly less if you've included some really "absorbing" things, such as small meat sandwiches, quiche, or miniature pasties.
- However, at a cocktail hour preceding a dinner party, serve lighter fare, no more than three to five pieces per guest, and make sure it goes on no longer than one hour prior to dinner. More than one hour will enable guests to eat or drink too much to do justice to the dinner that follows.
- If it is not possible to curtail the cocktail hour, season your dinner more highly to compensate for palates that may be dulled by alcohol.

*(continued on next page)*

*(continued from previous page)*

- Don't go overboard in your variety of predinner hors d'oeuvres—stick with a limited amount contingent on the amount of guests. For example, two types of hors d'oeuvres, each yielding a dozen and a half, augmented by a cheese or pâté spread is a sufficient amount of appetizers for a cocktail hour preceding a dinner party for eight people.

*Drinks*

- The cardinal rule of bartending is *Never run out of ice.* Over-buy lots of fresh ice, in a form that is manageable —that is, no large frozen clumps of ice cubes.
- When stocking your bar, always purchase more than you'll need. In many cases, you can negotiate the return of unused liquor with your supplier, if necessary. Liquor amounts are based on one jigger per drink (1.5 ounces); a glass of wine is four ounces. Assume three drinks before a dinner, four drinks at a cocktail party. Here is a guide to use in ordering your stock.

*LIQUOR (measured in fifths)*

| *no. of guests* | *average no. of drinks at cocktail hour* | *no. of bottles to buy* | *average no. of drinks at cocktail party* | *no. of bottles to buy* |
|---|---|---|---|---|
| 4 | 12 | 1 | 16 | 1 |
| 6 | 18 | 2 | 24 | 2 |
| 8 | 24 | 2 | 32 | 2 |
| 12 | 36 | 3 | 48 | 3 |
| 20 | 60 | 4 | 80 | 5 |
| 40 | 120 | 8 | 160 | 10 |

*WINE (measured in single 750 ml. bottles)*

| *no. of guests* | *average no. of glasses at cocktail hour* | *no. of bottles to buy* | *average no. of glasses at cocktail party* | *no. of bottles to buy* |
|---|---|---|---|---|
| 4 | 12 | 2 | 16 | 3 |
| 6 | 18 | 3 | 24 | 4 |
| 8 | 24 | 4 | 32 | 5 |
| 12 | 36 | 6 | 48 | 8 |
| 20 | 60 | 10 | 80 | 12 |
| 40 | 120 | 19 | 160 | 25 |

*(continued on next page)*

*(continued from previous page)*

- On the average, a guest will consume two drinks per hour.
- If you buy quarts of alcohol rather than fifths, you'll gain an additional four jiggers, or six ounces.
- Have your glassware—sparkling clean—set up at the location where you will do your bartending, either on a tray or arrayed on the counter. Also have at the ready your ice, cocktail napkins, stirrers, jiggers and barware, cut lemons and limes, olives, etc. for garnish. Stocking a bar area thus saves needed time and energy in the running of a party.
- Make sure the air is fresh and temperature controlled. A lot of people in one place create heat; you may wish to compensate by lowering the temperature to a point somewhat below that of which you would otherwise be comfortable.

realize the logistics of wassail-serving was the least of our concerns.

The open kitchen was U-shaped, with a small prep island in the center. On every horizontal plane were provisions for the party. Grocery bags of vegetables lined the floors, and cases of wine and champagne formed a short half-wall between the kitchen and dining room. The refrigerator was crammed solid with perishables. But nothing—*nothing!* was finished, or even in the initial stages of preparation.

With guests due to arrive in three hours, Kim and I gaped at the sight.

"Oh, uh, sorry; I've got everything for all the things I want to do, but I just ran out of time," Mrs. Farrell said, flustered. "But all the recipes are here in this book, marked with yellow post-it notes. If you could just make as much as possible . . . ?"

For the next three hours straight we worked like maniacs, clearing the table, setting up a buffet and mini bar (which I was supposed to tend), assembling scores of hors d'oeuvres, and plating them. As guests began to arrive, I got back into my tux jacket and left Kim to continue to assemble as many more of the recipes as she could.

For nearly six hours, with guests underfoot ("Hi, I brought my special tapenade; Elaine says to put it out. Do you have a bowl?"), new things continued to come out of the kitchen. They were no longer from the marked recipes; rather they were innovative creations born of the necessity of Getting Things Out, Now. Shrimp meant to have been butterflied and wrapped in blanched snow peas were instead layered over crushed ice and served with a tangy mayonnaise and horse-radish sauce. Pâté meant to be softened and piped onto thin slices of apples was instead served as a canapé with a slice of cherry tomato and capers. Still it seemed that no matter how much food we sent out we barely made a dent in the mounds of provisions on the countertops and in the refrigerator.

When the pace of food depletion slowed to a trickle, I called a halt to the production in the kitchen, and we went into maintenance and clean-up mode. An hour after the guests left, the kitchen was clean, all the food put away, everything organized.

"You were really *wonderful.* And weren't those recipes *great?"* gushed Mrs. Farrell, as we prepared to go. In addition to our hourly wages, she "tipped" us a cheeseball, part of the nondepleted refrigerator stores.

"How many recipes *did* she have marked?" I asked Kim as we drove home, exhausted, at midnight.

"Almost forty—each making at least thirty-six appetizers."

# 13

# The Long Road Home

As the scope of my contract butlering engagements grew, it led inevitably into catering. Because local zoning regulations prohibited me from running a full-scale catering operation from my home, I formed an alliance with a small, elegant French restaurant owned by a chef whose food I very much admired. I solicited the jobs and worked with the clients to plan the party and create the menu. Chef James provided the majority of the prepared food, which I then delivered and served. For the most part I concentrated on cocktail parties, smaller dinner parties, and corporate lunches.

The first party I did in conjunction with Chef James was for a client named Mrs. MacInnis, for whom I had previously done two smaller dinner parties. It was, she said, to be a large surprise party for her husband's fortieth birthday. She very much wanted an "over the hill" type of theme, a buffet with lots of seafood, a band, and a dance floor. Given these lofty aspirations, her modest budget presented a challenge.

We discussed ideas for a theme. Remembering the surprising popularity of the suggestive party favors at Mr. Carstairs',

I rather laughingly suggested setting the party up as a wake, mourning the demise of Mr. MacInnis' libido.

"Oh, that's *great*!" she exclaimed. "Everything in black, very funereal. Maybe even a coffin!"

Oh dear. Well, I was in for it now. Working with Chef James, we created a menu that met with her approval and fell within her means. But, since the party would be held in a tent, there wasn't the room nor the money for a dance band. We could use a disk jockey, but then I remembered a recent party I had attended where the hosts had hired a jukebox. The jukebox came set up with the sort of music the client wanted, and it accepted no money. It was a lot less intrusive than a DJ, and a lot more fun. Mrs. MacInnis agreed.

The arrangements for the party went swimmingly. I ordered the jukebox, set up with a variety of dance tunes from the fifties and sixties, which the rental company promised to transport to the party site early on the morning of the party. I arranged to hire a coffin from a prop house some miles away. Unfortunately, they didn't deliver. So, on the day before the party, after I oversaw the delivery and set-up of the tent, tables, and chairs, I left to pick up the coffin.

Conscious of wanting to save money wherever possible, I had not hired a van for the pickup; instead, the proprietor and I loaded the shiny black casket into the back of my Honda Accord hatchback. Of course, the length exceeded that of the hatchback. We tied the obligatory red flag to one of the pallbearer's handles and, after making sure the box was securely tied down, I set off.

I wonder that I didn't cause a traffic accident that Friday afternoon. Traffic slowed dramatically as I drove carefully down the heavily traveled freeway, the somber black coffin sticking out of the back of my car at a jaunty angle. In my rear-view mirror I saw people stop dead—no pun intended—and point at me, mouths agape. After a few minutes, I began to see the funny side of the whole situation, and started laughing, which added another incongruous note to the whole picture for those watching. I sunk low in my seat,

### Hints on Hiring Staff When Throwing a Party

- Use a reputable caterer, one you've met with, on site, on at least one occasion prior to the party. Develop a good working relationship with open communication lines. Know exactly which of you is supplying what; leave nothing to chance.
- In planning the party with the caterer, you will determine aspects such as the location of the kitchen, catering stations (if needed), back-up beverages, washing-up area, garbage, and recycled-goods bins. But make sure to cover such often-overlooked details as: Will the food be served from your platters, or from the caterer's? With whose serving utensils? Are there enough of them, and where are they located? Who will supply the coffee, in what, and are there sugar bowls and creamers? These small details count!
- Always anticipate the unexpected—have candles, etc., on hand for power failures and let the caterer know the location of fuseboxes and other back-up systems. On a less dramatic note, have a spare service (dinner set-up: plates, silverware, napkin, etc.) or two at hand for unforeseen guests.
- Go through every detail of what you expect to happen in half-hour segments. Then, while requesting to be kept informed, delegate the implementation to the caterer *and let him or her handle it.* Give the caterer clear directions as regards timing so that he or she can schedule the staff precisely—for example: "Pass hors d'oeuvres until 7:30, then clear; light candles and fill water glasses at 7:45; have the starter on the table when guests are seated at 7:55."
- For dinner parties where extra staff is being hired to set up and serve, set a sample place setting with the linen, china, silver, and crystal you want utilized. This example will ensure the rest of the table is laid exactly as you want it.

*(continued on next page)*

*(continued from previous page)*

- Have someone designated at the door to greet the guests and direct them to where they might leave coats. If the theme of the party is such that guests are likely to bring gifts, have a table or area ready where the gifts will be on display. Have the staff member keep a list of the gifts by writing the name of the giver on the numbered list, and sticking a round label with the corresponding number on the package.
- With a large number of guests and hired staff, use a coat-check system. Ideally, a coat check should be staffed by someone you know, but if that isn't possible, make sure only one person handles the chore, and make the coat-check area inaccessible to others.
- In handling a coat check, you can rent rolling garment racks with hangers, and label the hangers. Or, many large estates use lining tickets preprinted with the name of the house—a system easily adapted to a private house where you plan on laying out coats on a bed. Lining tickets are numbered tickets that are attached to the interior liner of the coat with an alligator clip—never a pin!—so as not to mar the exterior, which might be suede, silk, or fur. Coats are then folded with the interior uppermost, and laid out in numerical order with tickets exposed.
- Never stack coats. If, when retrieving a coat, others slide and things spill out of the pockets, it is a nightmare.
- In running a party, keep track of who is in what room, who came in, and who is leaving. Let staff know which rooms are open to guests and which are off limits, and ask that they help enforce it.
- If your party is for more people than your driveway will hold, talk to the local police department in advance to see if an off-duty officer can help with valet parking. Not only are they often very helpful, it is good public relations and extra security.

assumed my best impression of Jack Nicholson's sinister grin in "The Shining," and imagined I had a peel-and-stick car door sign that read "Joe's Undertaking: We Bury 'Em Deep, And Do It Cheap."

The jukebox arrived the day of the party. As we decorated the tent for the party, we sampled the selection of music. Chubby Checker, Elvis, Little Richard, the Ink Spots—all seemed to sound great.

"How about 'Honky Tonk Woman'?" one of the crew asked, as he pressed the buttons. *Plick, whirr, plop* went the jukebox, selecting the appropriate forty-five record and placing it on the turntable.

And then . . . nothing.

Oh no. I didn't need a malfunctioning jukebox five hours before the party was to start. After fiddling with it to no avail, I called the rental company.

"Go into the back of it, and hit the reset," they told me.

I did, and the needle swung over the turntable and settled onto the record. The rhythmic bass notes of "Honky Tonk Woman" filled the tent. I breathed a sigh of relief. Unfortunately, however, after the record ended, each subsequent request we made resulted in the same malfunction. The record would be transferred to the turntable, but the needle wouldn't follow.

Back and forth went the phone calls to the rental company, as I tried to fix the jukebox long-distance. The hours ticked away, closer and closer to the start of the party.

"This is ridiculous," I told the owner of the rental company. "I can't detail someone to reset the jukebox after every single song. Get me out a new jukebox, fast."

"Well, uh, I can bring you another, but unfortunately, by me time I get there, we won't have time to stock it with the music you wanted."

"What's in it now?"

"Country and western."

Bless her, Mrs. MacInnis took the music in stride. Everything was in readiness as the first of the guests began to arrive at dusk. A marquee congratulating Mr. MacInnis on his birthday stood outside the glowing tent. Inside, black and silver helium balloons adorned the poles and each table; tablecloths were silver lamé with black topcloths and napkins. Along the back of the tent were buffet tables filled with food and drinks.

An ice sculpture formed the base for the seafood bar, where in addition to large tiger prawns, there was a plethora of oysters on the half-shell, crab legs, and smoked salmon appetizers. Elsewhere, one table featured three different types of curry and the condiments— golden raisins, sliced bananas, diced cucumbers, plain yogurt, various chutneys, and grated coconut—while another held a cornucopia of fresh vegetables and dips, platters of sliced meats and cheeses, and small rolls for do-it-yourself finger sandwiches. Skewers of Thai chicken satay, cheese beignets, two types of quiche, and gallantine of duck on toast rounds were passed by me and the uniformed restaurant staff I had hired for the evening.

In the center of the tent near the dance floor stood the gleaming black casket. Silver balloons were tied to its chrome rail handles. Draped artlessly over its open lid were a set of black lace stockings, a garter belt, and a sexy push-up bra; on the pillow lay a spray of what appeared to be red roses, but were in actuality rolled-up red lace panties. (I made sure all of the lingerie was in Mrs. MacInnis' size.) We piled the quilted white satin interior high with the gifts brought by well-wishers.

Seventy people squeezed onto the tiny rented dance floor, hooting, stomping, and singing to country and western classics such as "Stand by Your Man" and "Mama, Don't Let Your Babies Grow Up to Be Cowboys." The dancing continued until after 1 A.M.

Even though the music substitution turned out to be a success, I used the failure of the first jukebox to extract a favor. When the owner's son pulled up in his van to collect it the following day, I confronted him. "You owe me one, mate," I told him.

"We're so sorry, Mr. Allen, about the jukebox," he said, his young face wretched. "I—we—don't know what we can do."

"Well, I know what you can do," I said, as sternly as possible. Then, with a smile, I clapped him on the shoulder. "There's plenty of room in your van. Take the coffin back for me, eh?"

The largest and most challenging party we ever did was for a national convention of recreational-vehicle owners. Over a four-day period, we provided buffet-style breakfasts and dinners and barbecue lunches. But the last night was to be the finale—a formal sit-down dinner for all two hundred attendees. What made its implementation a challenge was that the dinner was to be held under a tent on a beach, with no electricity or running water.

For the meal I had engaged Kim and six other wait-staff to help set up, serve, and break down the party. The tent, complete with tables and chairs, heaters, battery-powered lighting, and full flooring over temporary sub-flooring had been set up earlier. Rented china and crystal arrived shortly after we did, and against a backdrop of golden sand edged by the gentle swell of the tide, we set the tables with crisp white linen and sparkling china. Napkins were folded into wineglasses, adding height and visual impact to the tables.

Behind and to one side, another tent was erected, which we would use for preparation and serving. It was small—ten foot square—but was large enough to contain a bank of narrow tables down each side and a camp stove at the end. One side contained a row of banquet-sized chafing dishes, while the other side was strictly for prep. Although Chef James was providing the meal, it would be "finished"—plated—on site. And, a last-minute addition by the client—prior to the dinner, we would be serving hors d'oeuvres, which we needed to make there.

Between the hours of four and six, working as an assembly-line, the staff and I put together nearly one thousand hors d'oeuvres. At 6 P.M., while the sun set majestically over the water, we began serving the morsels, which included smoked salmon canapés stuffed with a horseradish and dill mayonnaise, cucumber boats stuffed with crab salad, and small spicy sausages rolled in hot, buttery, flaky pastry.

Returning to the prep tent for another tray of appetizers, I met Kim on her way out. "It's getting dark in there. Where do we find the lights for the prep tent?"

The lights for the prep tent . . . ? Oh, bloody hell!

"Eric," I called to one of the waiters, a tall, gangly youth of seventeen. "You're the tallest of any of us, and I need you to do something for me." Back in my car I had a large emergency lantern. "Would you get the lantern and stand over there—over near the stove, holding this up while we work?"

"Okay," the shy boy agreed. And for the next four hours, shifting from one aching arm to another, he stood like our own personal Statue of Liberty, illuminating the darkness.

At seven o'clock, on schedule, one of Chef James's staff arrived with the portable insulated containers known to caterers as Cambros. These contained all of the entrée components in their cooked, but unadorned, state. From the Cambros we transferred the dishes to the chafing dishes, which we had lit in readiness. The chafing dishes kept the meal hot as we served the first course, a simple green salad dressed with a raspberry vinaigrette.

Forming an assembly line once again, we began to plate the food and take it out. The meal, Tournedos Harlequin, was beautiful. It consisted of two beef medallions served over a layer of pâté on toast rounds. One tournedo was topped with a béarnaise sauce, the other with a rich Burgundy gravy. The tournedos were served with glazed baby carrots, creamed spinach, and roasted red potatoes with rosemary. We worked quickly, and to my satisfaction, had all two hundred people served within fifteen minutes.

Dessert was a special commemorative layer cake, decorated to resemble a large RV. After a speech by the client, two of the staff and I cut and served the cake, while the others cleared the tables. Then we began the process of cleaning up. Belatedly I realized that with no running water, much less hot water, clean-up was going to present a real challenge.

Feeling like campers, we carried water in buckets to the

prep tent where blessed Eric, his face stoic below his sore arms, still held the emergency lantern high above the prep area. On the stove we boiled water in our one large pot, and added new Sterno fuel cans to the chafing dishes in an effort to heat some water.

Fortunately, when dishes are rented, they simply have to be rinsed of any food debris before being returned. Even so, with three plates and three glasses per diner, we had a lot of rinsing to do. Still, triumphant from the many compliments we had received from the client and his guests, we were lighthearted about our primitive working conditions. With the pressure off, we relieved Eric of his torch duties to allow him to share in the joy of dishwashing.

It was late, nearly half-past eleven, when we finished packing up the party and I paid the wait-staff and sent them home. But regardless of the problems with the prep tent, I was exhilarated. I was working for myself, and it was starting to pay off.

When I closed my August books and ran a profit-and-loss analysis on the business three weeks later, the numbers bore out my exhilaration. Business was starting to pick up speed and we were turning a profit.

Yet a cloud hung on the otherwise sunny horizon—I was concerned about the future of my partnership with Chef James. In him I sensed reluctance; he wasn't convinced that a catering extension was a viable addition to his restaurant. We were scheduled to meet in the morning and go over some menus I wanted to present. I hoped the reports I had just run would help overcome his hesitation.

Another thing I was counting upon, for both our sakes, was the upcoming Christmas season. Weddings and holiday parties are the mainstay of successful catering firms, and I currently had two autumn weddings on the books, and was working on proposals for a few more. Late September—three weeks away—would begin the booking season for the holiday parties at year end, and I had my plans and advertizing all ready to capitalize on the period. A successful holiday season was critical to my becoming fully established as a caterer, and I felt strongly that it would reassure Chef James of our future prospects. I had started putting together a proposal for a winter wedding when the phone rang.

"Chris?" The feeble voice across the long-distance line was barely recognizable.

"Dad? What's the matter?"

"They've put me in hospital. It's cancer. You'd better come."

Kim held me wordlessly as I raged, my anger alternating with grief. "The doctor says its everywhere in his body." I could hear my voice break, and there seemed to be a crushing weight in my chest. "It could be a matter of weeks, or a few months. . . . Why does this all have to happen now? I have weddings and parties scheduled, and I'm finally beginning to make a name for myself as a caterer. What will happen to my credibility if I'm not here to follow through?"

Finally, emotions spent, I gave voice to my resolution. "I've got to go," I said.

"Yes, you do," she said. "Work will always be there, in some form or another. But your father won't be."

We flew to London four days later. Because I couldn't just sit at his bedside day after day and watch my father die, we came prepared to work on the Investment. I divided my time between there and the hospital and, of the two places, I found the house easier. Working fourteen-hour days, Kim, her father, my brother, and I stripped and cleaned walls, woodwork, and floors; and replaced heating and electrical systems, roof tiles, and bathroom and kitchen fixtures. But even as the condition of the Investment improved, my father's declined. Eight weeks after our arrival, he passed away.

With his passing, I felt my last ties to England had been severed. Taking a last look around, I put the now-restored house up for sale and left for home.

As I had feared, by the time I arrived home in late November, the large holiday parties I had hoped to book had been arranged elsewhere. Still, I worked up to Christmas, picking up whatever small parties I could find. Given the circumstances, the amount of business I had done had been acceptable, but far below what my expectations of the season had been prior to my sojourn in London. Thus it was that over the holidays, I found myself giving serious thought to my career.

It seemed that my responsibilities in England had always played a strong role in determining my future actions. I had gone into butlering to support my father and the house; the need for extensive repairs on the latter had influenced my switch to self-employment; now his death and the time spent in restoring and selling the house had led me to consider going back into a salaried position.

Shortly before New Year, Kim and I were having dinner in a quiet French restaurant when I brought up my dilemma.

"We need to discuss the future," I said.

"Whoa, this sounds heavy," Kim commented. "Have some more wine."

I waved away the proffered bottle. "Listen, I'm serious. I feel I'm at rather a fork in the road, but before I make a decision as to which direction I should head, I need your input.

"It's my belief that when I went to England, I lost critical momentum in really getting the catering operation going. Chef James was able to cover the jobs we had scheduled, but couldn't take it further than that. If I had been here, and we'd had a hugely busy holiday season, I think he'd be willing to keep going. But I know that, down deep, his heart is in the running of his restaurant. He isn't ready or willing to expand into the more full-scale operation that I envisage."

"I take it that he's talking about pulling out?" Kim said.

"He's making noises that way."

"Couldn't you find another restaurant?"

"No, I've thought about it." I fiddled with my napkin as I spoke. "I'm not interested in going into partnership with another restaurant. If I continue in this line, I want to get a loan and find a commercial property somewhere, where I can have my own kitchen. I want to control the end product, which, in this case, is the food."

"I see," Kim said cautiously. "What's the other direction?"

"Actually, I've been giving a lot of thought to going back into private service."

"Obviously, the subconscious choice."

"What do you mean?"

She indicated my napkin, which I had absently folded into a Bird of Paradise. "Could you really go back into service, after being self-employed?"

"Yes, but only if I can find what I want, which is to manage a large estate. And that's the rub, luv—almost certainly, such a position won't be found here." I knew relocating would be hard on my wife, who had never lived outside of her native California. Yet my domestic agency experience had verified there were few West Coast estates large enough to justify several live-in staff. California estates, as Mr. Carstairs had once noted, were based on the value of the land, not the sheer amount of it.

"Well," she said with visible apprehension, "it can't hurt to see what's out there."

As a butler is far from being a typical occupation, I suppose it should not be a surprise that getting a butler job can be far from conventional as well. Yet, even given the recollections of what had passed for interviews in every position I had held previously, I was totally unprepared for the one that resulted in my current position.

Regardless of locale, my professional contacts had assured me that someone with the sort of property for which I was looking would likely subscribe to the *New York Times*. As a result, I placed an ad in that publication's classified section outlining my qualifications, together with a description of what sort of a job I sought.

The eighth response to my advertisement was a gentleman who left a meandering ten-minute message on my answering machine. Kim and I listened to a well-modulated, agreeable voice expound on how he thought our objectives might be complementary. After we had played the tape back twice, she said, rather obscurely, "Well, he sounds *real,* that's for sure."

### Ten Things an Employer Should Know About the Successful Employment of Domestic Staff

1. Know what it is you wish the employee to do before you hire someone. Having a clear picture of exactly what the job description will entail, and communicating this clearly to a potential employee, will avoid misunderstandings.
2. Be clear and concise in your directions. If you have a tendency to forget things, ask that the employee write down your instructions, so that there is always a record of the request should a question arise.
3. Make sure that employees have the proper tools with which to do a job to your satisfaction. Let them know you hold them accountable for the tools given them.
4. In a house with multiple staff, there should be one person in charge—for example, a butler or estate manager. Deal with that person directly when there are problems with other employees, but otherwise, do not discuss one staff member with another.
5. Staff bedrooms should contain good beds and be of sufficient size to allow an employee to relax in comfort on his or her time off, particularly in the absence of a staff sitting room. Most of all, they should be off limits to you, unless there is an emergency. Employees have a right to their privacy.
6. Set high standards and adhere to them, but do not expect perfection beyond the ability of any other human being.
7. Remember to offer praise, not just criticism. Too many employers are quick to find fault and slow to commend a job well done. Employees will be far more content in their positions if they feel appreciated.
8. Never promise something—such as time off or a gratuity—then take it back. Memories are long and resentment goes deep.

*(continued on next page)*

*(continued from previous page)*

9. Be aware of the ramifications of special events, such as a late dinner party, when it falls on top of an already full day of work for a staff member. See that under such circumstances, he or she is given some time off during the day to rest or pursue his or her own activities.
10. Above all, remember that domestic employees are people, not automatons. They have feelings, hopes, ambitions, and lives of their own outside of their work. You will receive polite, respectful service by treating staff with courtesy and consideration.

The next morning I rang the gentleman at his office in New York City. "Oh, you're English," he said, when I introduced myself. "Oh, good. I love the English. I'm definitely an Anglophile."

When I asked him to tell me more about the position he had in mind, he described, in a rambling fashion, two properties he owned in the Hamptons on Long Island. One of them was undergoing a substantial remodel, and one of my main functions, for the duration of the construction, would be to act as a liaison between the project and him. My spirits rose. This sounded interesting.

I offered to FAX him my c.v. He seemed taken aback.

"Oh. I suppose that would be a good idea," he said. "Although I'm not sure we need to go into all of that. I feel really *right* about you."

That same day, several phone calls later, we were firming up plans for my coming to New York to spend a few weeks on the site as a sort of job trial, when he suddenly thought of something.

"What date is your birthday?"

Now it was my turn to be confused. Did he think I might be too young for the job?

"I'm thirty-five," I said.

"No, no. When is your birthday? I need to know, you see," he said.

Mystified, I told him.

He rang me back half an hour later. "I've had my astrologer in London run your numbers," he said jubilantly. "She agrees with me that you're *perfect.*"

I'd never gotten a job by heavenly means before. I thought it appropriate to thank my lucky stars.

For the past three years I have managed two large private estates in the Hamptons, almost on the very tip of Long Island. One, a five-bedroom "cottage," is my employer's private retreat. The other, for which my initial responsibility was to act as its general contractor, lies on adjacent property and was designed and built to be the most luxurious guest accommodations imaginable.

Set on over five landscaped acres of grounds, the 21,000 square-foot Greco-Italianate-style villa has eight bedrooms, each with its own telephone, television, and videocassette player. Marble bathrooms in each contain a steam shower and whirlpool bath. A sound system wired throughout the house allows the staff to change the ambiance easily via the background music.

Accoutrements for guests of the house include a tennis court, a croquet course, a rowboat for leisurely paddling on the large pond, and a swimming pool. Inside, there is a fully equipped movie theater capable of seating one hundred guests, a billiards room, and a complete gymnasium with television, stereo, and videocassette player (used, for example, for fitness video programs). A separate library elsewhere in the house contains the hundreds of videos available for visitors to borrow. An interior lap pool is equipped with the mechanics necessary to create a current into which visitors can swim as a form of exercise. Adjoining the interior pool area are a sauna, a steam room, and Swedish shower, as well as separate rooms containing a sun bed and a massage table. It's been compared to a spa, and it is—a private, extravagant getaway for his many friends and business acquaintances. My job is to see that they enjoy themselves.

In some ways it's a far cry from where I began. I am not permitted to wear a tuxedo while working; my employer deems it too stiff for the "country." I rarely have the opportunity to serve a formal dinner or afternoon tea. While my hours tend toward more daytime work than late evenings, it is still not unheard of for me to put in eighty-hour weeks during the summer and autumn seasons, dropping back to fifty hours during the winter and spring.

But adaptability will always be the key to success in my field, for the needs of each house, and every employer, are different. It makes for the variety that is a butler's job.

# 14

# Some Thoughts on Being a Butler

"We're a dying breed," an old servant once told me morosely, as I waited in the villa's staff room for Lady Welsh and Mr. Bristol to finish dinner. I thought differently at the time, and I still do.

Even in the low-key, back-to-basics 1990's, there is a job market out there for a butler, but not necessarily as the job is defined in Europe, and not just in large estates. Although the term "butler" seems to have more cachet, we would more accurately be titled "household executives," for like the eighteenth-century house steward, we are managers of all domestic affairs (and then some). Rather than being a diminishing species, domestic service could be a fledgling industry, for in today's hectic, fast-paced world, having such help is one way to enhance the quality of life.

The difficulty for those who would employ a household manager is finding one. My experience in running English Domestic Service Agency opened my eyes, not only to the business end of staff employment, but to the reality of what was available in the private service sector. I had expected that by focusing on the placement of only the executives of the domestic profession I would uncover other professionals with formal training. But after months of placing advertisements and networking with others in the trade, I came up against the frustrating fact that true "quality" staff were rare to the point of being on the brink of extinction. Predictably, those few maestros were firmly entrenched in jobs where they were well treated by their employers, and thus had no desire to leave.

It appeared to me that the whole industry was being eroded from the bottom up. Service was viewed as a job, not a career. Many of the potential employees I came across were immigrants with no formal training and only a limited command of the English language. They didn't know how to go the extra mile for their employer, and though some, like Jorge, whom I tutored on use of the *guéridon*, were willing to learn, there was no one to teach them. Without proper training, there was scant opportunity for advancement and, therefore, little, if any, loyalty. These workers would leave, often with no notice, for very little reason, but that reason, ninety-nine times out of one hundred, was money.

If there were adaptations to be made with the modern-day domestic employee, then so too were there adjustments for a new type of employer. "Old money" families were increasingly scarce; consequently, so were jobs in such households. However, the *nouveau riche*—defined as those who had made their money in the corporate world, often within the last generation—were on the rise. As I had learned with Mr. Carstairs, they had the means and the motivation to hire household managers. But many of these potential employers were unused to domestic staff, and thus inexperienced in their administration of them. Nor were they often prepared to pay them satisfactorily. When it became obvious that I would have to lower my standards and place lots of people of lower caliber in lots of jobs in which they would not last in order to be profitable, I closed the business.

As the old servants on the Côte d'Azur had said, few people seemed interested in going into service anymore. I believe that this is partly because there are fewer people available to train those who might choose to pursue such a career. Formal training was traditionally done through older servants in large, fully staffed houses, and the decline of these establishments has contributed in part to the dearth of professional personnel.

Perhaps, however, there's hope yet. Within the last several years schools in professional household management have appeared to teach someone the standards of formal domestic service. I am much cheered by this, for it is a worthy occupation in which one can do well and take much pride. Furthermore, as butlers/majordomos/household managers are a scarce commodity, the economic principle of supply and demand has its financial rewards.

My advice to those who employ, or wish to employ domestic staff is: *If you have or want good staff, pay them well!* Please do not deceive yourself; there are many other opportunities for competent domestic staff, which they will learn of, sooner or later.

I happened into butlering as a profession partly because it was the culmination of everything I then knew how to do. Having made that career move, I knew that I wanted to employ my talents in the United States, for two key reasons. First, I had heard that one could make better money as a top-level professional servant in America, whilst in England I knew that I would not earn much more than I had in the South of France. And second, my experience had indicated that a butler commanded a certain amount of respect in the United States—it seemed to be considered a genteel, albeit unusual, sort of way to make a living. I was a relic of an earlier age and, upon reflection, perhaps that wasn't such a bad thing. The Americans I had met in Europe looked on it as a status symbol; it brought them a certain amount of class to have an English butler, and by extension, to be one.

Here in America, with so many opportunities to make a good living open to those who wish to work, why would someone choose to go into a service position?

To those raised with American self-sufficiency, it is perhaps incomprehensible that anyone should choose, and

### Perfect Butlering

*General Maxims*

- Serve, but never be servile.
- The excuse "I can't" doesn't exist. Whatever your employer wants is *no trouble at all.* Be as helpful and accommodating as possible; for remember, it's a two-way street.
- Learn as many languages as possible. At the very least, learn the basics of three, including how to apologize, and how to ask where you might find a translator.
- Always try to improve your understanding of your employer's business.
- Read newspaper articles that are pertinent to your employer's business, hobbies, household, and personal habits. It not only keeps you current to what is going on in his industry, but it may allow you to offer a resource that he or she may not have known about. For example, an employer of mine had lost an old issue of a magazine I knew he collected. Because I had read, and made a notation of, an article in the *New York Times* about certain shops in New York City that hold back issues of every magazine, I was able to locate a copy of the missing issue and have it messengered to him within the hour.
- Read as many of your employer's books as possible, but not necessarily his copy. Go to the local library. Not only does it give you a handle on what sorts of things he's interested in, it allows you to converse with him on that subject. It also may give you insight into gift possibilities if people ask for suggestions.
- Never borrow your employer's things without his consent. Are you prepared to replace them and take the consequences?

*(continued on next page)*

*(continued from previous page)*

- Never lose your temper—not with other staff, and certainly not with a guest. Staying in control will prove that you have better manners. "Manners maketh the perfect servant."
- Maintain a current passport and inoculations at all times for last-minute travel purposes.

*Work habits*

- If your employer has a tendency to give a long list of multiple jobs each day, unless you are certain of what takes precedence, ask for his priorities.
- Try to complete one job before starting another.
- Make a list—daily or weekly, depending on your employer's style—and go over it with your employer. Date the list and keep it in a file. It not only helps you keep track of what you accomplish in a given day, but it helps to better define your job responsibilities when you update your c.v.
- If it is unavoidable that you call directory assistance rather than use the phone book, write the number down in your files for future use. Never give your employer cause to think that any of your habits are lazy.
- Every time you look up a telephone number, write it down in your files. Include on the notation why you called it—for example, "Specializes in repairing old windows."
- Keep your personal telephone directory separate from a house directory. The latter should contain the notations listed above. If you change jobs, you can give it to the next butler and make his life a lot easier, especially if he's from another area.
- Keep a good filing system. There are four possibilities for any piece of paper that comes into your possession:

*(continued on next page)*

*(continued from previous page)*

you can act on it (immediately), you can refer it to someone else to act on it, you can file it, or you can throw it away. Do not allow unnecessary clutter to build up.

- Always make sure you have two sets of every key you're given, and maintain a key log of who has what key. This is a security essential.
- Establish a local network with all suppliers and tradespeople as soon as possible. Ask for references.
- Insist that tradespeople make an appointment before they come to the house. Not only does it save you from wasting time, it shows you're serious about your professionalism and that you expect them to be too. Always let them know which entrance to use.
- Never leave tradespeople alone in the house, no matter how well you know them.
- Be cordial to all tradespeople. You never know for whom they'll work next.

*Proper distance*

- Never mix your personal life with your employer's life.
- Keep house accounts separate from your private checking account. Never borrow from the house account, but, conversely, do not permit a "float" of funds expended by you on behalf of your employer. Running his household is your job, but his fiscal responsibility.
- Never reveal too much of your life to your employer. He should never be considered your "buddy." He is your employer and can terminate you at any moment.
- When socializing with people outside of work, say little about your employer, and then only good things. You never know who you are talking to!

*(continued on next page)*

*(continued from previous page)*

- Seek your peers in other households, and always maintain a network of them. It is a small industry. Like Jeeves's infamous Book of the Junior Gannymede Club, which detailed the quirks of members' employers, such a network can alert you to certain people for whom you don't want to work.
- Insist on two regular days off per week. If you swap a day, go back to your regular two days as soon as possible, otherwise you'll end up losing them.
- Realize that if you do something once, it's a job for life.
- Always maintain a current curriculum vitae (résumé).

take pride in, a job that at its core, involves waiting on other people. While admittedly, I'm biased towards my job, I see no real disadvantages. After all, in what other profession can one enjoy a millionaire's lifestyle without being a millionaire?

As a butler, I've had the opportunity to travel around the world with and for my employers. I have lived in wonderful places, surrounded by beautiful things, where I have learned to appreciate the trappings of the very wealthy, including food, furnishings, clothing, and cars. I've had my daily meals prepared for me by world-class chefs, and driven luxurious vehicles. I have been the recipient of some incredible cast-offs by my employers, which have ranged from expensive clothing and shoes, to the Mini I bought for a song. My working clothes, whether a tuxedo in formal households or a navy blazer and khaki pants in those less so, are purchased for me by my employers, as is my health insurance. And, most importantly, my American employers have always been very appreciative of what I do for them, which is a source of great job satisfaction.

Is this a profession for everyone? Definitely not. It takes a particular "presence," but more than that, a singular attitude. It requires an credo of "surprise and delight"; service, but *not* servility. You do not submerge your personality, although you do keep a level of decorum and of distance from the family for whom you work. In serving, you are no less of a person than those you serve. A career as a butler or majordomo is little different from that of a private secretary, executive administrative assistant, or trusted protégé to, say, the chairman of the board in the corporate world.

If there are drawbacks outside of the long hours, they are these. First, you never truly shut off your work when you are off duty. Even out of the house, you still indirectly represent your employer, and must maintain a certain degree of decorum. Second, you are by nature of the job privy to many secrets that you may never discuss; it is your duty to guard your employers' privacy. (For example, names, places, and other salient details in this book have been changed or obscured so as to protect the privacy of my previous employers.) Third, your job is to ease their lives and ensure it runs as smoothly as possible. *Their* job is to continue to make the money to pay your not-insubstantial salary. All in all, I find it a pretty good trade-off.

William Tayler, an eighteenth-century gentleman's gentleman, wrote in his journal: "The life of a gentleman's servant is something like that of a bird shut up in a cage. The bird is well-housed and well fed but deprived of liberty, and liberty is the dearest and sweetest object of all Englishmen." But in that same entry he concluded: "If a person wish [*sic*] to see life, I would advise him to be a gentleman's servant. They will see high and low life, above stairs as well as life below. They will see and know more than any other class of people in the world."

I doubt I could say it better myself.

# Bibliography


Chester-Levy, Catherine. "Sir?" *Sotheby's Preview* 6, no. 6 (1991): 30–31.

Copeland, Ann Bellah. *Complete Housekeeping Book.* New York: Old Westbury Gardens, 1985.

Cotton, Leo, ed. *Old Mr. Boston's De Luxe Official Bartender's Guide.* Boston: Mr. Boston Distiller, Inc., 1935.

Drury, Elizabeth. *The Butler's Pantry Book.* New York: St. Martin's Press, 1981.

Ferguson, G. "Make My Day, Jeeves." *U.S. News & World Report* 112 (1992): 16–17.

Girouard, Mark. *Life in the English Country House: A Social and Architectural History.* New Haven: Yale University Press, 1978.

Hoge, S. K. "My Life as a Butler Working at the St. Regis Hotel, New York City." *Condé Nast Traveller* 27 (1992): 132–135.

Kenyon, Michael. "Almost Jeeves: Hunting for a Job in the Hamptons." *Gourmet* 47 (1987), 64.

———. "Not Quite Escoffier." *Gourmet* 48 (1987), 68.

Lee, J. "Steady, Jeeves, You've Got Company!" *U.S. News & World Report* 104 (1988), 52.

Lew, Julie. "Upstairs, Downstairs: A Way to Manage Both." *New York Times* (April 15, 1993): sec. C, p. 1.

Nelton, S. "Answering the Need for 'Refuge.'" *Nation's Business* 80 (1992), 14.

Post, Elizabeth L. *The New Emily Post's Etiquette.* New York: Funk & Wagnalls, 1975.

Schmidt, William E. "In Her Majesty's Service, But Without Free Soap." *New York Times* (October 2, 1993): sec. 1, p 3.

Seely, Lida. *Mrs. Seely's Cookbook.* New York: The MacMillan Company, 1902.

Smith, J. "What the Butler Knew." *Gentleman's Quarterly* 58 (1988), 63.

Story, R. D. "My Man Stocker." *New York* 23 (1990), 26.

Wolkomir, R. "Heads Up, Thumbs In: Butlers Learn How to Deliver the Goods." *Smithsonian* 18 (1988): 110–114.

This book was set by SkidType of Savannah, Georgia. Type designed by William Caslon in the early eighteenth century featured refinements on the Dutch faces that were currently in use. It immediately became very popular. Caslon's easy legibility and its availability, in its original form and many imitations, made it the type most widely used by job printers in America in colonial days, and, indeed, through most of the nineteenth century. Avoiding later cuttings, and adaptations made for machine typesetting, Carol Twombly returned to Caslon's early specimens for the digital version used in this book. She designed the face for Adobe Systems Incorporated.